Best of Fons&Porter®

S0-BYN-102

Easy Quilts

FONS & PORTER STAFF
Editors-in-Chief Marianne Fons and Liz Porter

Editor Jean Nolte
Assistant Editor Diane Tomlinson
Managing Editor Debra Finan
Technical Writer Kristine Peterson

Art Director Tony Jacobson

Editorial Assistant Cinde Alexander
Sewing Specialist Cindy Hathaway

Contributing Photographers Craig Anderson, Dean Tanner, Katie Downey
Contributing Photo Assistant DeElda Wittmack

Publisher Kristi Loeffelholz
Advertising Manager Cristy Adamski
Retail Manager Sharon Hart
Web site Manager Phillip Zacharias
Customer Service Manager Tiffiny Bond
Fons & Porter Staff Peggy Garner, Shelle Goodwin, Kimberly Romero, Laura Saner, Karol Skeffington, Yvonne Smith, Natalie Wakeman, Anne Welker, Karla Wesselmann

New Track Media LLC
President and CEO Stephen J. Kent
Chief Financial Officer Mark F. Arnett
President, Book Publishing W. Budge Wallis
Vice President/Publishing Director Joel P. Toner
Vice President, Circulation Nicole McGuire
Vice President, Production Derek W. Corson
Production Manager Dominic M. Taormina
Production Coordinator Kristin N. Burke
IT Manager Denise Donnarumma
New Business Manager Susan Sidler
Renewal and Billing Manager Nekeya Dancy
Online Subscriptions Manager Jodi Lee

Our Mission Statement
Our goal is for you to enjoy making quilts as much as we do.

LEISURE ARTS STAFF
Editor-in-Chief Susan White Sullivan
Quilt and Craft Publications Director Cheryl Johnson
Special Projects Director Susan Frantz Wiles
Senior Prepress Director Mark Hawkins
Imaging Technician Stephanie Johnson
Prepress Technician Janie Marie Wright
Publishing Systems Administrator Becky Riddle
Mac Information Technology Specialist Robert Young

President and Chief Executive Officer Rick Barton
Vice President and Chief Operations Officer Tom Siebenmorgen
Vice President of Sales Mike Behar
Director of Finance and Administration Laticia Mull Dittrich
National Sales Director Martha Adams
Creative Services Chaska Lucas
Information Technology Director Hermine Linz
Controller Francis Caple
Vice President, Operations Jim Dittrich
Retail Customer Service Manager Stan Raynor
Print Production Manager Fred F. Pruss

Library of Congress Control Number: 2011926083
ISBN-13/EAN: 978-1-60900-248-0

We hope you'll enjoy this collection of easy quilt patterns that can each be made in a weekend or less. Simplified patchwork, larger blocks, strip sets, and other shortcuts make it all possible without sacrificing beauty. While these quilts are a perfect starting point for beginning quilters, they are also great for more experienced quilters who are looking for projects that are quick to finish. As you browse through the pages, we think you'll find inspiration for your next quilt.

Happy quilting,

Marianne + Liz

Table of Contents

14

54

70

Techniques

76

100

128

146

QUILT DESIGNED BY **Michele Scott**.
MADE BY **Elinore Locke**. MACHINE QUILTED BY **Linda J. Hahn**.

Once Around the Block

Create a contemporary quilt with these boldly colored blocks that are fun to make.

Size: 58" × 82"

Blocks: 16 (12" × 18") blocks

MATERIALS

16 fat quarters★ assorted prints in red, orange, green, purple, and blue

1 yard red print for inner border and binding

⅜ yard each of purple, orange, blue, and green prints for outer border

5 yards backing fabric

Twin-size quilt batting

★fat quarter = 18" × 20"

NOTE: Fabrics in the quilt shown are from the Nature's Palette collection by Michele Scott for Northcott.

Cutting

Measurements include ¼" seam allowances. Border strips are exact length needed. You may want to make them longer to allow for piecing variations.

From red print, cut:

- 8 (2¼"-wide) strips for binding.
- 7 (1½"-wide) strips. Piece strips to make 2 (1½" × 72½") side inner borders and 2 (1½" × 50½") top and bottom inner borders.

From each fat quarter, cut:

- 3 (3½"-wide) strips. From strips, cut 4 (3½" × 6½") D rectangles and 4 (3½" × 4½") B rectangles.
- 3 (2½"-wide) strips. From strips, cut 4 (2½" × 6½") C rectangles and 8 (2½" × 3½") A rectangles.

From each purple and orange print, cut:

- 2 (4½"-wide) strips. Piece strips to make 1 (4½" × 74½") side outer border.

From each blue and green print, cut:

- 2 (4½"-wide) strips. Piece strips to make 1 (4½" × 58½") top or bottom outer border.

Block Assembly

1. Join matching C and D rectangles, matching A and B rectangles, and 1 A rectangle of a different color as shown in *Unit 1 Diagrams*. Make 32 Unit 1.

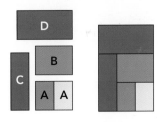

Unit 1 Diagrams

2. In the same manner, make 32 Unit 2 (*Unit 2 Diagram*).

Unit 2 Diagram

3. Lay out 2 Unit 1 and 2 Unit 2 as shown in *Block Assembly Diagram*. Join Units to complete 1 block *(Block Diagram)*. Make 16 blocks.

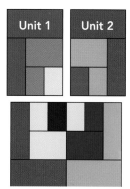

Block Assembly Diagram

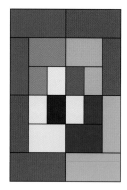

Block Diagram

Quilt Assembly

1. Lay out blocks as shown in *Quilt Top Assembly Diagram*. Join into rows; join rows to complete quilt center.

2. Add red print side inner borders to quilt center. Add red print top and bottom inner borders to quilt.

3. Repeat for outer borders.

Finishing

1. Divide backing into 2 (2½-yard) lengths. Cut 1 piece in half lengthwise to make 2 narrow panels. Join 1 narrow panel to each side of wider panel; press seam allowances toward narrow panels.

2. Layer backing, batting, and quilt top; baste. Quilt as desired. Quilt shown was quilted with an allover design *(Quilting Diagram)*.

3. Join 2¼"-wide red print strips into 1 continuous piece for straight-grain French-fold binding. Add binding to quilt.

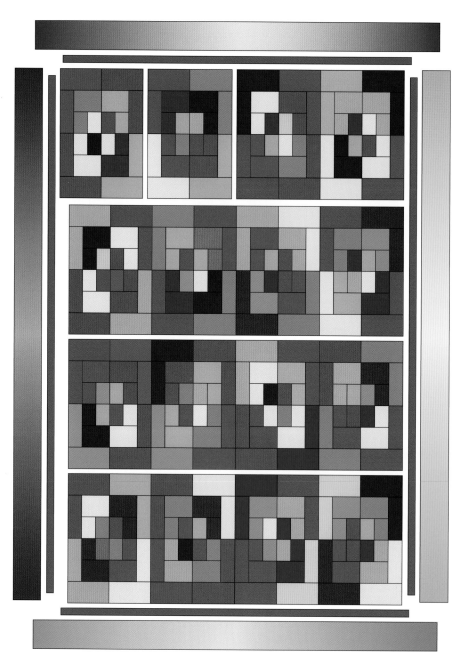

Quilt Top Assembly Diagram

Quilting Diagram

TRIED & TRUE

Dip into your stash of batik fat quarters to make another version of this quilt. Our blocks are made with Timeless Treasures batiks.

WEB EXTRA

Go to www.FonsandPorter. com/oncearoundtheblock-sizes to download *Size charts*, *Materials Lists*, and *Quilt Top Assembly Diagrams* for *Crib*, *Twin*, and *Queen* size options.

DESIGNER

Michele Scott is a teacher, lecturer, and quilt and fabric designer known for her outrageous personality. Michele lives in Center City, Philadelphia with her two dogs.

Contact her at: The Pieceful Quilter
1136 O'Neil Street
Philadelphia, PA 19123
(215) 627-2484
michele@piecefulquilter.com
www.piecefulquilter.com ✳

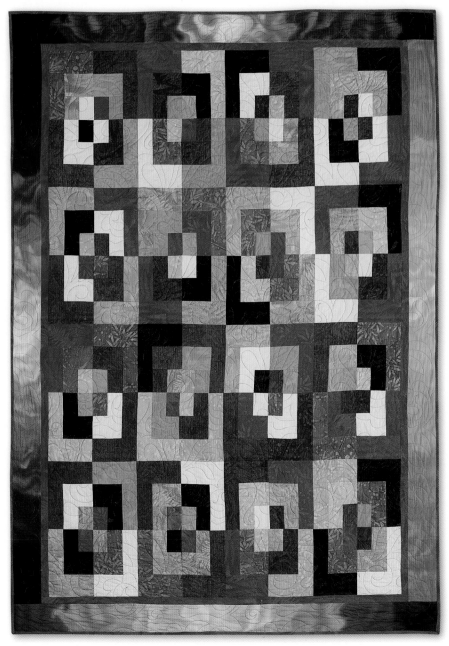

Checkerboard Twist

Bright squares of color bounce over a black-and-white checkerboard in this quilt designed by Mimi Wellington. It looks a bit tricky, but goes together quickly and easily.

Size: 43" × 55"
Blocks: 48 (6") blocks

MATERIALS

8 fat quarters★ assorted bright
   prints in yellow, purple, blue,
   green, pink, and red
1 yard black solid
1 yard white solid
⅝ yard black print for outer border
½ yard dark pink print for binding
2¾ yards backing fabric
Crib-size quilt batting
★fat quarter = 18" × 20"

Cutting

Measurements include ¼" seam allowances. Border strips are exact length needed. You may want to make them longer to allow for piecing variations.

From each print fat quarter, cut:
• 2 (5"-wide) strips. From strips, cut 6 (5") B squares.

From black solid, cut:
• 14 (2"-wide) strips. From 2 strips, cut 28 (2") A squares. Remaining strips are for strip sets.

From white solid, cut:
• 14 (2"-wide) strips. From 2 strips, cut 28 (2") A squares. Remaining strips are for strip sets.

From black print, cut:
• 6 (2½"-wide) strips. Piece strips to make 2 (2½" × 51½") side outer borders and 2 (2½" × 43½") top and bottom outer borders.

From dark pink print, cut:
• 6 (2¼"-wide) strips for binding.

Block Assembly

1. Join 2 black solid strips and 1 white solid strip as shown in *Strip Set #1 Diagram*. Make 4 Strip Set #1. From strip sets, cut 66 (2"-wide) #1 segments.

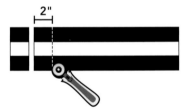

Strip Set #1 Diagram

2. Join 2 white solid strips and 1 black solid strip as shown in *Strip Set #2 Diagram*. Make 4 Strip Set #2. From strip sets, cut 66 (2"-wide) #2 segments.

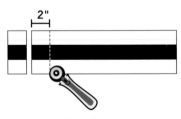

Strip Set #2 Diagram

3. Lay out 2 #1 segments, 1 white solid A square, and 1 print B square as shown in *Block 1 Assembly Diagram*. Join to complete 1 Block 1 *(Block 1 Diagram)*. Make 24 Block 1.

Block 1 Assembly Diagram

Block 1 Diagram

4. In the same manner, make 24 Block 2 using 2 #2 segments, 1 black solid A square, and 1 print B square in each *(Block 2 Diagrams)*.

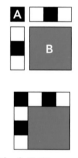

Block 2 Diagrams

Quilt Assembly

1. Lay out blocks as shown in *Quilt Top Assembly Diagram*. Join into rows, join rows to complete quilt center.

> ### Sew **Smart**™
> **Alternate Block 1 and Block 2 and turn blocks as shown to make the black-and-white checkerboard pattern surrounding the bright squares. —Liz**

2. Referring to *Quilt Top Assembly Diagram*, join 5 #1 segments, 5 #2 segments, 1 white solid A square, and 1 black solid A square to make 1 side inner border. Make 2 side inner borders. Add borders to sides of quilt center.

3. In the same manner, join 4 #1 segments, 4 #2 segments, 1 white solid A square, and 1 black solid A square to make top inner border. Repeat for bottom border. Add borders to quilt.

4. Add black print side outer borders to quilt center. Add top and bottom outer borders to quilt.

Finishing

1. Divide backing into 2 (1⅜-yard) lengths. Cut 1 piece in half lengthwise to make 2 narrow panels. Join 1 narrow panel to wider panel; press seam allowances toward narrow panels. Remaining panel is extra and can be used to make a hanging sleeve.

SIZE OPTIONS

	Crib (31" × 43")	Twin (67" × 97")	Full (85" × 97")
#1 Blocks	12	75	98
#2 Blocks	12	75	97
Setting	4 × 6	10 × 15	13 × 15

CUTTING

Bright Prints	8 fat eighths★	25 fat quarters	33 fat quarters
Black Solid	⅝ yard	2⅛ yards	2¾ yards
White Solid	⅝ yard	2⅛ yards	2¾ yards
Black Print	⅜ yard	¾ yard	⅞ yard
Binding Fabric	⅜ yard	¾ yard	⅞ yard
Backing Fabric	1⅜ yards	6 yards	7½ yards
Batting	Crib-size	Queen-size	Queen-size

★fat eighth = 9" × 20"

2. Layer backing, batting, and quilt top; baste. Quilt as desired. Quilt shown was quilted with an allover flower design *(Quilting Diagram)*.

3. Join 2¼"-wide dark pink print strips into 1 continuous piece for straight-grain French-fold binding. Add binding to quilt.

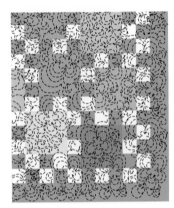

Quilting Diagram

WEB EXTRA

Go to www.FonsandPorter.com/cktwistsizes to download *Quilt Top Assembly Diagrams* for these size options.

DESIGNER

Mimi Wellington and her family live in Eagle, Idaho. When she's not designing and creating her own quilts, Mimi does custom quilting for others.

Contact her at:
Moon Over the Mountain
1197 S River Flow Way
Eagle, ID 83616
(208)938-9034
mimiwellington@msn.com ※

TRIED & TRUE

Create a calmer version using small prints in neutral tones such as these from the Bread & Butter collection by Whimsicals for Red Rooster Fabrics.

Fat Quarter Breeze

Layer fat quarters and cut big pieces for a
quilt you can make in no time.

Size: 59" × 74"

Blocks: 12 (15") blocks

MATERIALS

12 fat quarters★★ assorted batiks for
blocks

½ yard orange batik for inner
border

1¼ yards blue batik for outer border

6 fat eighths★ assorted batiks for
binding

3¾ yards backing fabric

Twin-size quilt batting

★fat eighth = 9" × 20"

★★fat quarter = 18" × 20"

Cutting

Measurements include ¼" seam
allowances. Border strips are exact
length needed. You may want to make
them longer to allow for piecing
variations.

From each fat quarter, cut:

NOTE: Refer to *Fat Quarter Cutting
Diagram* to cut pieces from fat quarters.

• 1 (10½"-wide) strip. From strip, cut 6
(3" × 10½") rectangles.

• 1 (5½"-wide) strip. From strip, cut 3
(5½") squares.

Sew **Smart**™

To speed up cutting, layer 3 or 4
fat quarters and cut as shown in
Fat Quarter Cutting Diagram. —
Marianne

Fat Quarter Cutting Diagram

From orange batik, cut:

- 6 (2½"-wide) strips. Piece strips to make 2 (2½" × 60½") side inner borders and 2 (2½" × 49½") top and bottom inner borders.

From blue batik, cut:

- 7 (5½"-wide) strips. Piece strips to make 2 (5½" × 64½") side outer borders and 2 (5½" × 59½") top and bottom outer borders.

From each assorted fat eighth, cut:

- 3 (2¼"-wide) strips for binding.

Block Assembly

1. Place fabric rectangles and squares in 9 stacks and number the stacks as shown in *Stack Diagrams*. Maintain the same fabric order in each stack.

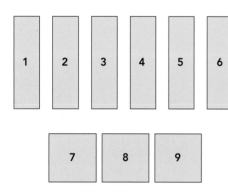

Stack Diagrams

2. Remove top rectangle from stack #2 and place it on bottom of the stack. Remove top 2 rectangles from stack #3 and place them on bottom. Remove top 3 rectangles from stack #4 and place them on bottom. Repeat for all remaining stacks in this manner, increasing by 1 the number of pieces moved to the bottom of each successive stack.

3. Join top rectangle from each of stacks #1–#4 to make Unit A *(Unit A Diagram)*. Make 12 Unit A.

Unit A Diagram

4. Join top rectangle from each of stack #5 and #6 to make Unit B *(Unit B Diagram)*. Make 12 Unit B.

Unit B Diagram

5. Join top square from each of stack #7–#9 to make Unit C *(Unit C Diagram)*. Make 12 Unit C.

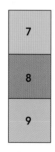

Unit C Diagram

6. Join 1 Unit A, 1 Unit B, and 1 Unit C as shown in *Block Diagrams*. Make 12 blocks.

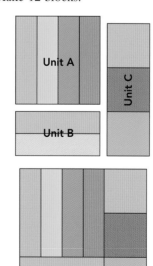

Block Diagrams

Quilt Assembly

1. Lay out blocks as shown in *Quilt Top Assembly Diagram*. Join into rows; join rows to complete quilt center.

2. Add side inner borders to quilt center. Add top and bottom inner borders to quilt.

3. Repeat for outer borders.

Finishing

1. Divide backing into 2 (1⅞-yard) lengths. Join panels lengthwise. Seam will run horizontally.

2. Layer backing, batting, and quilt top; baste. Quilt as desired. Quilt shown was quilted with an allover design *(Quilting Diagram)*.

3. Join 2¼"-wide binding strips into 1 continuous piece for straight-grain French-fold binding. Add binding to quilt.

Quilting Diagram

Quilt Top Assembly Diagram

TRIED & TRUE

We used soft and sweet
1930s reproduction fabrics
by Nancy Mahoney for
P&B Textiles to create an
old-fashioned quilt like
grandma used to make!

SIZE OPTIONS

	Twin (74" × 89")	Queen (89" × 104")	King (104" × 104")
Blocks	20	30	36
Setting	4 × 5	5 × 6	6 × 6
CUTTING			
Fat Quarters	20	30	36
Orange Batik	⅝ yard	⅝ yard	¾ yard
Blue Batik	1½ yards	1¾ yards	1⅞ yards
Binding Fabric	⅝ yard	¾ yard	⅞ yard
Backing Fabric	5½ yards	8 yards	9½ yards
Batting	Full-size	Queen-size	King-size

Twin Size

Queen Size

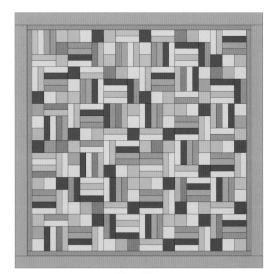

King Size

DESIGNER

Butch Myers took up quilting to keep busy when he quit smoking. Since then, he has made dozens of quilts. We're saddened by the fact that since he made this quilt, Butch has passed away. ✳

Flip a Coin

This beautiful, simple-to-sew quilt is a contemporary version
of a traditional pattern called Chinese Coins.

Size: 60½" × 69"

MATERIALS

1¼ yards multi-color stripe

2 yards blue floral

12 fat eighths★ assorted prints in
green, blue, orange, and red

½ yard orange print for binding

3¾ yards backing fabric

Twin-size quilt batting

Borders Made Easy® tear away
pattern (optional)

★fat eighth = 9" × 20"

NOTE: Fabrics in the quilt shown are
from the Linden collection designed by
Melissa Saylor for P&B Textiles.

Cutting

Measurements include ¼" seam allowances.

From each fat eighth, cut:

- 4 (2"-wide) strips for strip sets.

From multi-color stripe, cut:

- 19 (2¼"-wide) strips. Piece strips to
make 10 (2¼" × 69½") strips.

From blue floral, cut:

- 4 (7½" × 69½") **lengthwise** strips.

From orange print, cut:

- 7 (2¼"-wide) strips for binding.

Quilt Assembly

1. Join 4 assorted print strips as shown
in *Strip Set Diagram.* Make 12 strip
sets. From strip sets, cut 60 (3½"-wide)
segments.

3½"

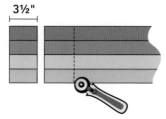

Strip Set Diagram

2. Referring to *Quilt Top Assembly
Diagram* on page 22, join 12 strip set
segments. Remove 2 rectangles to
make center of 1 Strippy Row. Add
1 stripe strip to each side of center
to complete 1 Strippy Row. Make 5
Strippy Rows.

3. Lay out Strippy Rows and blue floral
strips as shown in *Quilt Top Assembly
Diagram.* Join rows to complete quilt
top.

Finishing

1. Divide backing fabric into 2 (1⅞-yard)
lengths. Join panels lengthwise. Seam
will run horizontally.

2. Layer backing, batting, and quilt top;
baste. Quilt as desired. Quilt shown
was machine quilted using Borders
Made Easy® Cable design #111 in
the floral rows, in the ditch between
rows, and with Xs in the Strippy
Rows *(Quilting Diagram).*

3. Join 2¼"-wide orange print strips
into 1 continuous piece for straight-
grain French-fold binding. Add binding
to quilt.

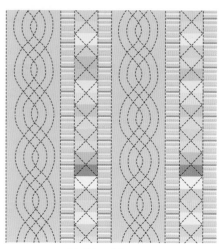

Quilting Diagram

TRIED & TRUE

Pick any dramatic large-scale print for the wide vertical strips. In this version, Michele used Kaffe Fassett fabrics from Westminster.

Strippy Row

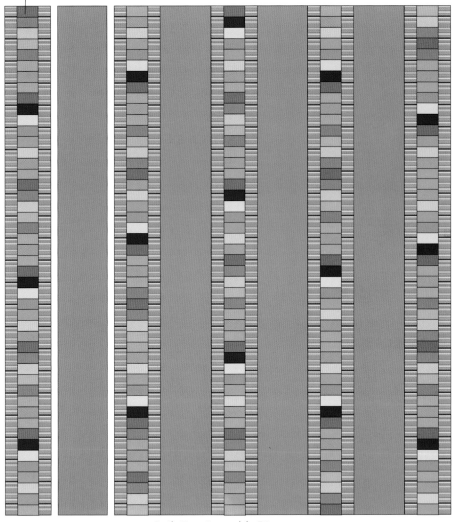

Quilt Top Assembly Diagram

WEB EXTRA

Go to www.FonsandPorter.com/coin sizes to download *Quilt Top Assembly Diagrams* for these size options.

SIZE OPTIONS

	Crib (33½" × 45")	Queen (87½" × 99")	King (101" × 105")
Strippy Rows	3	7	8
"Coins" in each row	30	66	70
Floral Rows	2	6	7
CUTTING			
Fat Eighths	5	24	28
Stripe	½ yard	2¼ yards	2¾ yards
Blue floral	¾ yard	3⅜ yards	4 yards
(cut strips crosswise and piece)			
Binding	⅜ yard	¾ yard	¾ yard
Backing Fabric	1½ yards	7⅞ yards	9 yards
Batting	Crib-size	Queen-size	King-size

DESIGNER

Idaho quilter Michele Sorensen loves to work with color. She especially enjoys the quilt design process and interacting with other quilters.

Contact Michele at: sorensen_michele@yahoo.com ✳

Sunset

This contemporary crazy quilt is easy to make with a collection of bold prints in a monochromatic color scheme.

Size: 38" × 64"

MATERIALS

⅜ yard dark red print for side inner border

⅞ yard bright red print for outer border

⅝ yard red stripe for binding

¼ yard each of 17 assorted red prints for blocks

1½ yards muslin or lightweight non-fusible interfacing for block foundations

2 yards backing fabric

Crib-size quilt batting

NOTE: Fabrics in the quilt shown are from the Sunset collection by Paintbrush Studio for Fabri-Quilt, Inc.

Cutting

Measurements include ¼" seam allowances. Border strips are exact length needed. You may want to make them longer to allow for piecing variations.

From dark red print, cut:

• 2 (1½"-wide) strips. From strips, cut 2 (1½" × 36½") side inner borders.

From bright red print, cut:

• 5 (4½"-wide) strips. From strips, cut 2 (4½" × 38½") top and bottom borders. Piece remaining strips to make 2 (4½" × 56½") side outer borders.

From red stripe, cut:

• 6 (2¼"-wide) strips for binding.

From each assorted red print and remainder of dark red print, bright red print, and red stripe, cut:

• Irregular strips in varying widths from 1½"–5" (*Cutting Diagram*).

> **Sew Smart™**
>
> If you want to cut strips that are wider at one end than the other, open the folded fabric and cut from selvage to selvage.
> —Marianne

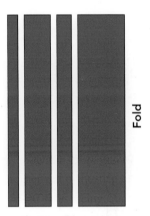

Fold

Cutting Diagram

From muslin, cut:

• 4 (7½" × 36½") A rectangles.

• 2 (10½" × 30½") B rectangles.

Block Assembly

1. Place 1 red print strip, right side up, at an angle on muslin A rectangle. Ends of strip should extend slightly beyond edge of base rectangle (*Block Assembly Diagrams* on page 26).

2. Place another red print strip atop first red strip, right sides facing, aligning one long side. Stitch strips together, stitching through foundation.

3. Press second red print strip open.

4. Continue adding red print strips, angling as shown in *Block Assembly*

Block Diagram

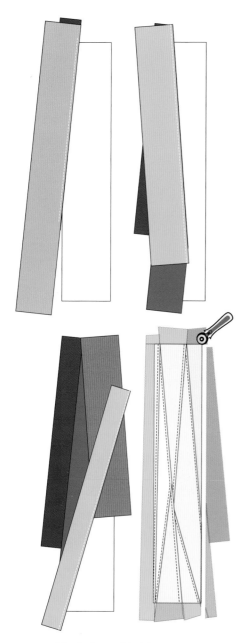

Block Assembly Diagrams

Diagrams, until entire muslin rectangle is covered.

Sew **Smart**™

As you make blocks, don't be concerned if each strip doesn't cover the muslin base from end to end. The greater variety of angles, the more your block will look like a crazy-pieced block. For more efficient use of red strips, cut some into shorter lengths.—Liz

5. Trim edges of strips even with edges of foundation rectangle to complete 1 block A *(Block Diagram).* Make 4 Block A.

6. In the same manner, make 2 block B using muslin B rectangles and remaining red print strips.

Quilt Assembly

1. Lay out 4 Block A as shown in *Quilt Top Assembly Diagram.* Join blocks to complete quilt center.

2. Add dark red print side inner borders to quilt center.

Quilt Top Assembly Diagram

3. Add 1 block B to top of quilt. Add remaining block B to bottom of quilt.

4. Add bright red side outer borders to quilt. Repeat for top and bottom outer borders.

Finishing

1. Layer backing, batting, and quilt top; baste. Quilt as desired. Quilt shown was quilted with a different freehand design in each piece and meandering in the border *(Quilting Diagram)*.

2. Join 2¼"-wide red stripe strips into 1 continuous piece for straight-grain French-fold binding. Add binding to quilt.

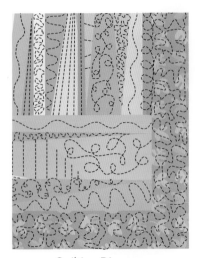

Quilting Diagram

DESIGNER

Shawn York started quilting in 2000. She lives in southern California with her husband and three children. Shawn loves scrappy, primitive quilts, and managed to blend old-style crazy quilting and the contemporary look of the Sunset fabric into a modern, easy quilt.

Contact her at: 6949 Elfin Oaks Road • Elfin Forest, CA 92029 • 760-752-7784 • shawn@rustycrow.com
www.RustyCrowQuiltShop.com ✳

Nouveau Bargello

Bargello patchwork, inspired by needlepoint "flame" patterns, is not difficult to sew. You'll make simple strip sets, cut the sets into various-width segments, then combine into a beautiful, allover design.

Size: 35¼" × 42½"

MATERIALS

8 fat quarters★ in 2 or 3 color families in solids or prints in a range of values from light to dark.

NOTE: Combining these values is what gives the contrast necessary for a successful bargello quilt. Vary the scale of the prints on your fabrics.

¼ yard black solid for inner border

1 yard black stripe for outer border

⅜ yard red print for binding

1⅜ yards backing fabric

Crib-size quilt batting

★fat quarter = 18" × 20"

NOTE: Fabrics in the quilt shown are from the Tulip Nouveau collection by Ro Gregg for Northcott.

Cutting

Measurements include ¼" seam allowances. Arrange your selected fat quarters in an attractive sequence, blending color families from light to dark. Number fabrics in this sequence #1–#8.

From each fat quarter, cut:

• 4 (2½"-wide) strips.

From black solid, cut:

• 4 (1¼"-wide) strips. From strips, cut 2 (1¼" × 32½") side inner borders and 2 (1¼" × 26¾") top and bottom inner borders.

From black stripe (positioning stripe the same on each), cut:

• 4 (5"-wide) strips for outer border.

From red print, cut:

• 5 (2¼"-wide) strips for binding.

Quilt Assembly

1. Referring to *Photo A*, arrange 8 assorted strips in numbered order. Join strips to make a strip set. Repeat to make 4 strip sets. Press seam allowances up in 2 strip sets, and down in 2 strip sets *(Photo B)*.

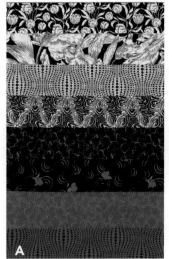

Fabric 1
Fabric 2
Fabric 3
Fabric 4
Fabric 5
Fabric 6
Fabric 7
Fabric 8

A

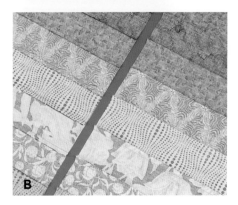

B

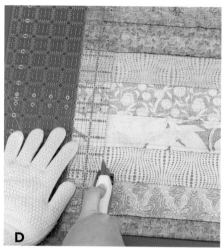

2. Join 2 strips sets with seams pressed up as shown. Stitch top and bottom edges together to make Tube A *(Photo C)*. Press seams in same direction as others. In the same manner, join remaining 2 strip sets with seams pressed down to make Tube B.

3. Position Tube A on flat rotary cutting surface. Referring to *Cutting Table*, cut tube into loops the widths indicated *(Photo D)*. **Number these loops and keep them in order.**

CUTTING TABLE

Loop	Tube A	Tube B
#1	2"	1¾"
#2	1½"	1¼"
#3	1"	¾"
#4	1"	1¼"
#5	1½"	2"
#6	2½"	3"
#7	2½"	2"
#8	1½"	1"
#9	¾"	1"
#10	1¼"	1½"
#11	2"	1½"
#12	1¼"	1"

4. In the same manner, cut tube B into loops. **Number loops and keep in order.**

Sew Smart™

For ease in assembly, label loops with sticky notes as you cut. —Liz

5. Remove stitches between fabric #1 and the one above it (fabric #8) in loop A1. Place strip right side up on flat surface, with fabric #1 at the top *(Photo E)*.

6. Remove stitches between fabric #2 and fabric #1 in loop B1. Place strip B1 next to strip A1, with fabric #2 at the top.

7. Continue removing stitches in loops, referring to *Stitching Chart* and *Quilt Top Assembly Diagram* on page 31 to determine which stitches to remove and which fabric will be at top of strip.

8. Join strips as shown in *Quilt Top Assembly Diagram* to complete quilt center.

9. Add black side inner borders to quilt center. Add top and bottom inner borders to quilt.

10. Add outer borders to quilt, mitering corners.

Finishing

1. Layer backing, batting, and quilt top; baste. Quilt as desired. Quilt shown was machine quilted with variegated thread in curved lines which emphasize the flow of colors *(Quilting Diagram)*.

2. Join 2¼"-wide red stripe strips into 1 continuous piece for straight-grain French-fold binding. Add binding to quilt.

Quilting Diagram

Sew Smart™

Instructions for mitering borders can be downloaded at FonsandPorter.com/mborders. —Marianne

STITCHING CHART

STRIP # →																							
A1	B1	A2	B2	A3	B3	A4	B4	A5	B5	A6	B6	A7	B7	A8	B8	A9	B9	A10	B10	A11	B11	A12	B12
1	2	3	4	5	6	5	4	3	2	1	8	7	6	5	4	3	4	5	6	7	8	1	2
2	3	4	5	6	7	6	5	4	3	2	1	8	7	6	5	4	5	6	7	8	1	2	3
3	4	5	6	7	8	7	6	5	4	3	2	1	8	7	6	5	6	7	8	1	2	3	4
4	5	6	7	8	1	8	7	6	5	4	3	2	1	8	7	6	7	8	1	2	3	4	5
5	6	7	8	1	2	1	8	7	6	5	4	3	2	1	8	7	8	1	2	3	4	5	6
6	7	8	1	2	3	2	1	8	7	6	5	4	3	2	1	8	1	2	3	4	5	6	7
7	8	1	2	3	4	3	2	1	8	7	6	5	4	3	2	1	2	3	4	5	6	7	8
8	1	2	3	4	5	4	3	2	1	8	7	6	5	4	3	2	3	4	5	6	7	8	1
1	2	3	4	5	6	5	4	3	2	1	8	7	6	5	4	3	4	5	6	7	8	1	2
2	3	4	5	6	7	6	5	4	3	2	1	8	7	6	5	4	5	6	7	8	1	2	3
3	4	5	6	7	8	7	6	5	4	3	2	1	8	7	6	5	6	7	8	1	2	3	4
4	5	6	7	8	1	8	7	6	5	4	3	2	1	8	7	6	7	8	1	2	3	4	5
5	6	7	8	1	2	1	8	7	6	5	4	3	2	1	8	7	8	1	2	3	4	5	6
6	7	8	1	2	3	2	1	8	7	6	5	4	3	2	1	8	1	2	3	4	5	6	7
7	8	1	2	3	4	3	2	1	8	7	6	5	4	3	2	1	2	3	4	5	6	7	8
8	1	2	3	4	5	4	3	2	1	8	7	6	5	4	3	2	3	4	5	6	7	8	1

FABRIC # →

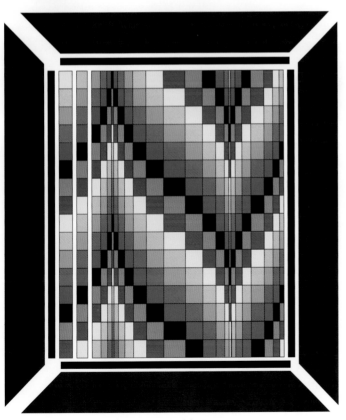

Quilt Top Assembly Diagram

TRIED & TRUE

We used Bali Batiks in shades of blue, green, and purple to make our version of this spectacular quilt.

DESIGNER

Patti Carey enjoys playing with new fabrics and designing quilts that inspire other quilters.

Contact Patti at:

patti.carey@northcott.net ❋

QUILT AND PILLOWS DESIGNED AND MACHINE QUILTED BY **Jean Nolte**.

MADE BY **Diane Ide**.

Simply Strippy
Throw and Pillows

You can make this simple quilt in just a few hours. Use a bit more time and fabric to create toss pillows to match!

Throw

Size: 49½" × 71½"

MATERIALS

NOTE: Fabrics in the quilt shown are from the Running 8ths collection by Springs Creative.

2⅝ yards strippy fabric (If not using Running 8ths fabric, you will need 1⅞ yards each of 8 prints. Use remainders of prints to make pillows.)

¾ yard brown solid for inner border and binding

3½ yards backing fabric

Twin-size quilt batting

Cutting

Measurements include ¼" seam allowances.

From strippy fabric, cut:

• 1 (60½"-long) piece. From piece, cut 8 (5¼"-wide) **lengthwise** strips.

From remainder of strippy fabric, cut:

• 8 (5¼"-wide) **lengthwise** strips. Piece strips to make 2 (5¼" × 62½") side outer borders and 2 (5¼" × 50") top and bottom outer borders.

From brown solid, cut:

• 7 (2¼"-wide) strips for binding.

• 6 (1½"-wide) strips. Piece strips to make 2 (1½" × 60½") side inner borders and 2 (1½" × 40½") top and bottom inner borders.

Quilt Assembly

1. Referring to *Quilt Top Assembly Diagram* on page 34 and photo, join strips to complete quilt center.

2. Add brown side inner borders to quilt center. Add brown top and bottom inner borders to quilt.

3. Repeat for pieced outer borders.

Finishing

1. Divide backing fabric into 2 (1¾-yard) lengths. Join pieces lengthwise. Seam will run horizontally.

2. Layer backing, batting, and quilt top; baste. Quilt as desired. Quilt shown was quilted with overlapping 8½" circles, 3¼" circles, and with parallel lines in the outer border (*Quilting Diagram*).

3. Join 2¼"-wide brown strips into 1 continuous piece for straight-grain French-fold binding. Add binding to quilt.

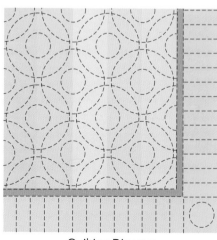

Quilting Diagram

SIZE OPTIONS

	Twin (63¾" × 94½")	Full (82¾" × 94½")
Center Strips	11	15
Strippy Fabric	4¾ yards	6 yards
Brown solid	1 yard	1⅛ yards
Backing Fabric	5¾ yards	7½ yards
Batting	Full-size	Queen-size

CUTTING

Strippy Fabric	11 (5¼" × 83½") **lengthwise** strips for center	15 (5¼" × 83½") **lengthwise** strips for center
	5 5¼" × 65") **lengthwise** strips for outer border	8 (5¼" × 45") **lengthwise** strips for outer border
Brown Solid	8 (1½"-wide) strips for inner border	9 (1½"-wide) strips for inner border
	9 (2¼"-wide) strips for binding	10 (2¼"-wide) strips for binding

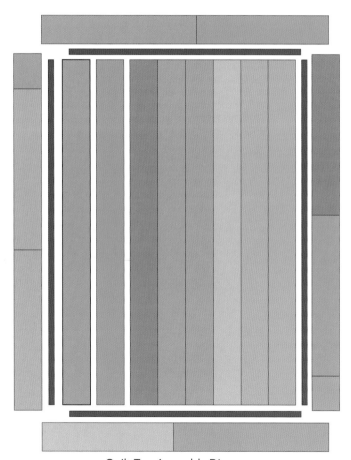

Quilt Top Assembly Diagram

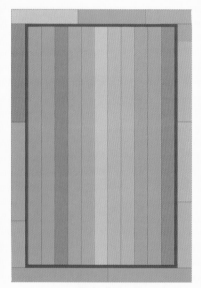

Twin Size

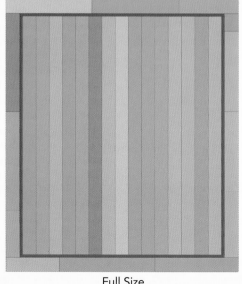

Full Size

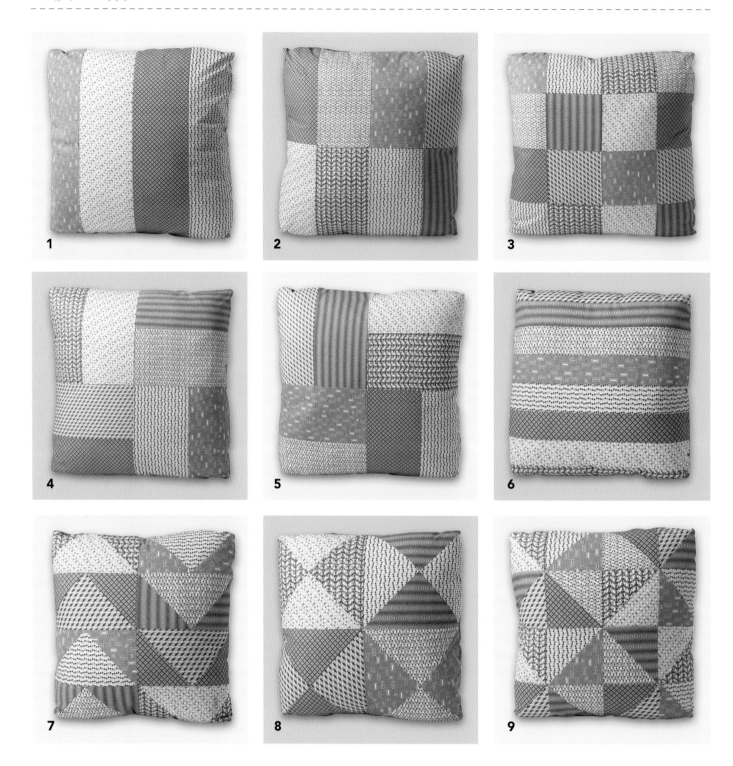

*Simple patchwork toss pillows are easy to make and
quickly add warmth and beauty to your room décor.*

Pillows

Sizes:
Pillows #1–#5 19" × 19"
Pillows #6–#9 16" × 16"

MATERIALS

Pillow #1:
⅝ yard strippy fabric (will make 2 pillows)
Pillows #2, #3, #4, and #5:
⅜ yard strippy fabric for each pillow
Pillow #6:
½ yard strippy fabric (will make 2 pillows)
Pillows #7, #8, and #9:
⅝ yard strippy fabric for each pillow
Backing for each Pillow:
¾ yard
Fons & Porter Half & Quarter Ruler
Pillow Form

Cutting

Measurements include ¼" seam allowances. Instructions are written for using the Fons & Porter Half & Quarter Ruler. See *Sew Easy: Cutting Half-Square and Quarter-Square Triangles* on page 39. **NOTE:** If not using the Fons & Porter Half & Quarter Ruler, make a 9¼" square template. Cut square in half diagonally in both directions to make 4 quarter-square triangles. Use 1 triangle for quarter-square triangle template. Follow Notes for cutting half-square triangles.

For pillow #1, cut:
• 4 (5¼" × 19½") strips.
For pillow #2, cut:
• 8 (5¼" × 10") strips.

For pillow #3, cut:
• 8 (5¼" × 10½") strips. From each strip, cut 2 (5¼") squares.
For pillow #4, cut:
• 8 (5¼" × 10") strips.
For pillow #5, cut:
• 8 (5¼" × 10") strips.
For pillow #6, cut:
• 8 (2½" × 16½") strips.
For pillow #7, cut:
• 8 (4½"-wide) **lengthwise** strips. From light strips, cut 8 quarter-square triangles. From dark strips, cut 16 half-square triangles. **NOTE:** If not using the Fons & Porter Half & Quarter Ruler, cut 8 (4⅞") dark squares. Cut squares in half diagonally to make 16 half-square triangles.
For pillow #8, cut:
• 8 (4½"-wide) **lengthwise** strips. From each strip, cut 2 quarter-square triangles.
For pillow #9, cut:
• 8 (4½" × 18") strips. From each strip, cut 4 half-square triangles. **NOTE:** If not using the Fons & Porter Half & Quarter Ruler, cut 2 (4⅞") squares. Cut squares in half diagonally to make 4 half-square triangles.
From backing fabric, cut:
For pillows #1–#5:
• 2 (19½" × 25") rectangles.
For pillows #6–#9:
• 2 (16½" × 21") rectangles.
From backing fabric for each pillow #1–#5:
• 2 (23" × 19½") rectangles.
From backing fabric for each pillow #6–#9:
• 2 (20" × 16½") rectangles.

Pillow #1

1. Join strips as shown in *Pillow #1 Diagram*.

Pillow #1 Diagram

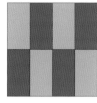
Pillow #2 Diagram

Pillow #3 Diagram

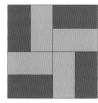
Pillow #4 Diagram

2. Finish pillow as described in *Sew Easy: Pillow Finishing* on page 38.

Pillow #2

1. Join strips as shown in *Pillow #2 Diagram*.
2. Finish pillow as described in *Sew Easy: Pillow Finishing* on page 38.

Pillow #3

1. Join squares in rows, alternating dark and light. Join rows as shown in *Pillow #3 Diagram*.
2. Finish pillow as described in *Sew Easy: Pillow Finishing* on page 38.

Pillow #4

1. Join 2 strips to make a square. Make 4 squares. Join squares, keeping lighter strips in center as shown in *Pillow #4 Diagram*.
2. Finish pillow as described in *Sew Easy: Pillow Finishing* on page 38.

Pillow #5

1. Join 2 strips to make a square. Make 4 squares. Join squares, keeping darker strips in center as shown in *Pillow #5 Diagram* on page 38.
2. Finish pillow as described in *Sew Easy: Pillow Finishing* on page 38.

Sew *Easy*

Pillow Finishing

Use this quick and easy method to make the back for your throw pillow.

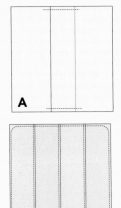

A

B

1. Fold each piece of backing fabric in half crosswise, wrong sides facing; press.
2. Overlap pressed edges, making a square the same size as pillow top. Baste overlapped edges together (*Diagram A*).
3. Place pillow top atop backing, right sides facing. Stitch around outer edge (*Diagram B*).

Sew **Smart**™
Slightly round the corners when stitching to avoid sharp points on the finished pillow. —Marianne

4. Turn right side out through opening in pillow back. Insert pillow form inside pillow cover.

Pillow #5 Diagram

Pillow #6 Diagram

Flying Geese Unit Diagrams

Pillow #7 Diagram

Pillow #6
1. Join strips as shown in *Pillow #6 Diagram*.
2. Finish pillow as described in *Sew Easy: Pillow Finishing*.

Pillow #7
1. Join 2 dark half-square triangles and 1 light quarter-square triangle to make 1 Flying Geese Unit (*Flying Geese Unit Diagrams*). Make 8 Flying Geese Units. Join 4 Flying Geese Units into a row. Make 2 rows. Join rows as shown in *Pillow #7 Diagram*.
2. Finish pillow as described in *Sew Easy: Pillow Finishing*.

Hourglass Unit Diagrams

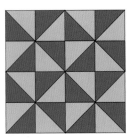
Pillow #8 Diagram

Triangle-Square Diagrams

Pinwheel Diagram

Pillow #9 Diagram

Pillow #8
1. Join 2 matching dark quarter-square triangles and 2 matching light quarter-square triangles to make 1 Hourglass Unit (*Hourglass Unit Diagrams*). Make 4 Hourglass Units.
2. Join Hourglass units as shown in *Pillow #8 Diagram*.
3. Finish pillow as described in *Sew Easy: Pillow Finishing*.

Pillow #9
1. Join 1 light half-square triangle and 1 dark half-square triangle to make a triangle-square (*Triangle-Square Diagrams*). Make 16 triangle-squares.
2. Join 4 triangle-squares to make 1 Pinwheel (*Pinwheel Diagram*). Make 4 Pinwheels. Join 4 Pinwheels as shown in *Pillow #9 Diagram*.
3. Finish pillow as described in *Sew Easy: Pillow Finishing*.

Cutting Half-Square and Quarter-Square Triangles

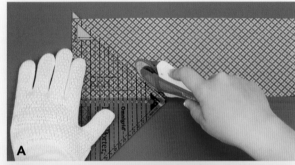

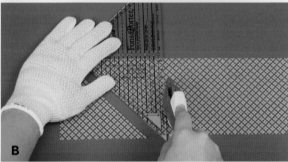

Easily cut triangles for *Simply Strippy Pillows* from strips of the same width.

Cutting Half-Square Triangles

1. Straighten the left edge of 4½"-wide fabric strip. Place the 4" line of the Fons & Porter Half & Quarter Ruler on the bottom edge of strip, aligning left edge of ruler with straightened edge of strip. The yellow tip of ruler will extend beyond top edge of strip.
2. Cut along right edge of ruler to make 1 half-square triangle (*Photo A*).
3. Turn ruler and align 4" line with top edge of strip. Cut along right edge of ruler (*Photo B*).
4. Repeat to cut required number of half-square triangles.

Cutting Quarter-Square Triangles

1. Place Fons & Porter Half & Quarter Ruler on 4½"-wide fabric strip, with 4" line along bottom edge. The black tip of ruler will extend beyond top edge. Trim off end of strip along left edge of ruler.
2. Cut along right edge of ruler to make 1 quarter-square triangle (*Photo C*).
3. Turn ruler and align 4" line along top edge of strip. Cut along right edge of ruler (*Photo D*).
4. Repeat to cut required number of quarter-square triangles.

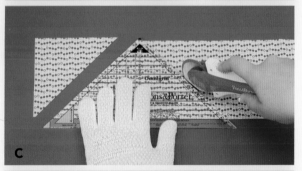

Serendipity

This quilt is so simple, yet so charming.
All you need is five of your favorite fabrics, and you're ready go.
It will be done in an afternoon!

Size: 54" × 72"

MATERIALS

1⅜ yards dark brown print
1 yard brown circle print
⅝ yard blue dot print
¾ yard blue tree print
1 yard cream floral print
3½ yards backing fabric
Twin-size quilt batting

NOTE: Fabrics in the quilt shown are from the Fusions, Mingle, and Night and Day collections by Robert Kaufman Fabrics.

Cutting

Measurements include ¼" seam allowances.

From dark brown print, cut:
- 3 (9½"-wide) strips. From 1 strip, cut 2 (9½" × 18½") B rectangles. From remaining strips, cut 2 (9½" × 24½") A rectangles and 2 (9½" × 12½") C rectangles.
- 7 (2¼"-wide) strips for binding.

From brown circle print, cut:
- 3 (9½"-wide) strips. From strips, cut 2 (9½" × 24½") A rectangles, 1 (9½" × 18½") B rectangle, and 1 (9½" × 12½") C rectangle.

From blue dot print, cut:
- 2 (9½"-wide) strips. From strips, cut 3 (9½" × 18½") B rectangles, and 1 (9½" × 12½") C rectangle.

From blue tree print, cut:
- 1 (24½"-wide) strip. From strip, cut 1 (24½" × 9½") A rectangle, and 3 (18½" × 9½") B rectangles.

From cream floral print, cut:
- 3 (9½"-wide) strips. From strips, cut 1 (9½" × 24½") A rectangle, 3 (9½" × 18½") B rectangles, and 2 (9½" × 12½") C rectangles.

Quilt Assembly

1. Lay out rectangles as shown in *Quilt Top Assembly Diagram*.

2. Join rectangles into vertical rows; join rows to complete quilt top.

Finishing

1. Divide backing into 2 (1¾-yard) lengths. Join panels lengthwise. Seam will run horizontally.

2. Layer backing, batting, and quilt top; baste. Quilt as desired. Quilt shown was quilted with an allover floral design *(Quilting Diagram)*.

3. Join 2¼"-wide dark brown print strips into 1 continuous piece for straight-grain French-fold binding. Add binding to quilt.

Quilting Diagram

Quilt Top Assembly Diagram

Sweetwater

You can make this easy quilt in an evening! This simple design works well with any assortment of fat quarters—brights, reproductions, batiks, juvenile prints, or 1930s prints.

Size: 66" × 66"
Blocks:
16 (13") blocks

MATERIALS

7 fat quarters★ assorted prints in green and black

10 fat quarters★ assorted prints in cream and tan

¾ yard green print for blocks and inner border

1½ yards cream print for blocks and outer border

¾ yard black solid for binding

4 yards backing fabric

Twin-size quilt batting

★fat quarter = 18" × 20"

NOTE: Fabrics in the quilt shown are from the Authentic collection by Sweetwater for Moda Fabrics.

Cutting

Measurements include ¼" seam allowances. Border strips are exact length needed. You may want to make them longer to allow for piecing variations.

From each green and black print fat quarter, cut:

- 1 (9½"-wide) strip. From strip, cut 2 (9½") A squares.
- 1 (4½"-wide) strip. From strip, cut 2 (4½") B squares.

From each cream and tan print fat quarter, cut:

- 2 (4½"-wide) strips. From strips, cut 3 (4½" × 9½") C rectangles.

From green print, cut:

- 1 (9½"-wide) strip. From strip, cut 2 (9½") A squares and 2 (4½") B squares.
- 6 (2"-wide) strips. Piece strips to make 2 (2" × 55½") top and bottom inner borders and 2 (2" × 52½") side inner borders.

From cream print, cut:

- 7 (6"-wide) strips. Piece strips to make 2 (6" × 66½") top and bottom outer borders and 2 (6" × 55½") side outer borders.
- 1 (4½"-wide) strip. From strip, cut 2 (4½" × 9½") C rectangles.

From black solid, cut:

- 8 (2¼"-wide) strips for binding.

Block Assembly

1. Lay out 1 A square, 1 B square, and 2 C rectangles as shown in *Block Assembly Diagram*.

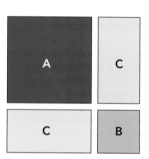

Block Assembly Diagram

2. Join into rows; join rows to complete 1 block (*Block Diagram*). Make 16 blocks.

Block Diagram

Quilt Assembly

1. Lay out blocks as shown in *Quilt Top Assembly Diagram*. Join into rows; join rows to complete quilt center.

2. Add green print side inner borders to quilt center. Add top and botttom inner borders to quilt.

3. Repeat for cream print outer borders.

Finishing

1. Divide backing into 2 (2-yard) lengths. Cut 1 piece in half lengthwise to make 2 narrow panels. Join 1 narrow panel to each side of wider panel; press seam allowances toward narrow panels.

2. Layer backing, batting, and quilt top; baste. Quilt as desired. Quilt shown was quilted with overlapping circles (*Quilting Diagram*).

3. Join 2¼"-wide black strips into 1 continuous piece for straight-grain French-fold binding. Add binding to quilt.

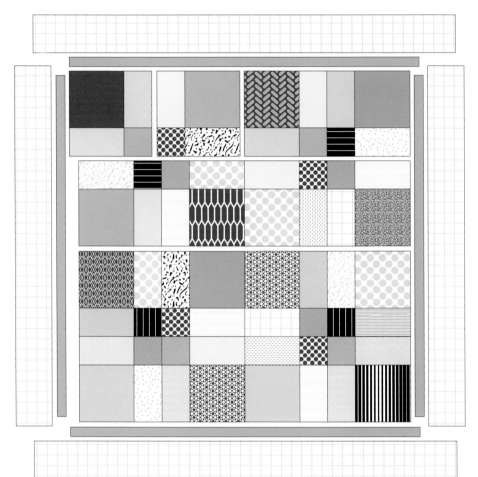

Quilt Top Assembly Diagram

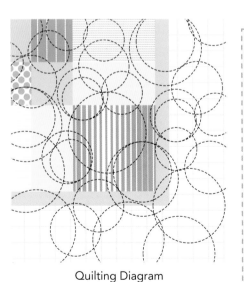

Quilting Diagram

TRIED & TRUE

We used cozy flannel prints from the Warm Winter Wishes collection by Cheryl Seslar for Northcott in our block.

SIZE OPTIONS

	Twin (66" × 92")	Full (79" × 92")	Queen (92" × 105")
Blocks	24	30	42
Setting	4 × 6	5 × 6	6 × 7

MATERIALS

	Twin (66" × 92")	Full (79" × 92")	Queen (92" × 105")
Green and Black Prints	12 fat quarters	15 fat quarters	21 fat quarters
Cream and Beige Prints	8 fat quarters	10 fat quarters	14 fat quarters
Green Print	⅞ yard	1 yard	1 yard
Cream Print	1½ yards	1⅝ yards	1⅞ yards
Black Solid	¾ yard	¾ yard	1 yard
Backing Fabric	5½ yards	7½ yards	8¼ yards
Batting	Full-size	Full-size	King-size

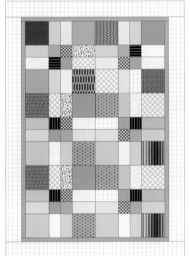

Twin Size

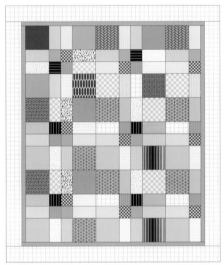

Full Size

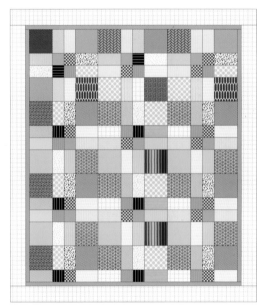

Queen Size

QUILT DESIGNED BY **Toadusew Creative Concepts**.
MADE BY **Colleen Reale**. MACHINE QUILTED BY **Chloe Anderson**.

Sassy Stripes

Easy strip piecing makes stitching this quilt a breeze!

Size: 54" × 72"
Blocks: 48 (9") blocks

MATERIALS

NOTE: Fabrics in the quilt shown are from the Bleeker Street collection by Marcus Brothers.

¾ yard blue dot
1 yard green dot
¾ yard dark blue print
¾ yard dark green print
½ yard dark stripe
1 yard light stripe
½ yard light blue print
½ yard light green print
3½ yards backing fabric
Twin-size quilt batting

Cutting

Measurements include ¼" seam allowances.

From blue dot, cut:

- 14 (1½"-wide) strips for strip sets.

From green dot, cut:

- 14 (2"-wide) strips for strip sets.

From dark blue print, cut:

- 3 (4"-wide) strips for strip sets.
- 6 (2"-wide) strips for strip sets.

From dark green print, cut:

- 3 (4"-wide) strips for strip sets.
- 6 (2"-wide) strips for strip sets.

From dark stripe, cut:

- 2 (4"-wide) strips for strip sets.
- 4 (2"-wide) strips for strip sets.

From light stripe, cut:

- 2 (4"-wide) strips for strip sets.
- 4 (2"-wide) strips for strip sets.
- 7 (2¼"-wide) strips for binding.

From light blue print, cut:

- 2 (4"-wide) strips for strip sets.
- 4 (2"-wide) strips for strip sets.

From light green print, cut:

- 2 (4"-wide) strips for strip sets.
- 4 (2"-wide) strips for strip sets.

Block Assembly

1. Join 2 (2"-wide) dark stripe strips, 1 (2"-wide) green dot strip, 1 (1½"-wide) blue dot strip, and 1 (4"-wide) dark stripe strip as shown in *Strip Set #1 Diagram* on page 50. Make 2 Strip Set #1. From strip sets, cut 6 (9½"-wide) #1 segments.

2. Join 2 (2"-wide) dark blue print strips, 1 (2"-wide) green dot strip, 1 (1½"-wide) blue dot strip, and 1 (4"-wide) dark blue print strip as

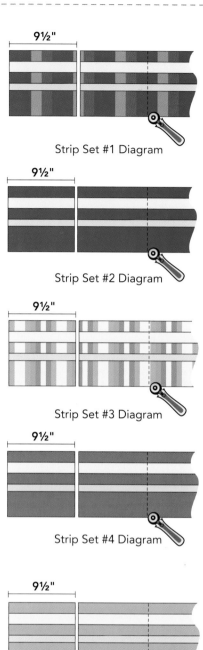

9½"

Strip Set #1 Diagram

9½"

Strip Set #2 Diagram

9½"

Strip Set #3 Diagram

9½"

Strip Set #4 Diagram

9½"

Strip Set #5 Diagram

9½"

Strip Set #6 Diagram

shown in *Strip Set #2 Diagram*. Make 3 Strip Set #2. From strip sets, cut 12 (9½"-wide) #2 segments.

3. Join 2 (2"-wide) light stripe strips, 1 (2"-wide) green dot strip, 1 (1½"-wide) blue dot strip, and 1 (4"-wide) light stripe strip as shown in *Strip Set #3 Diagram*. Make 2 Strip Set #3. From strip sets, cut 6 (9½"-wide) #3 segments.

4. Join 2 (2"-wide) dark green print strips, 1 (2"-wide) green dot strip, 1 (1½"-wide) blue dot strip, and 1 (4"-wide) dark green strip as shown in *Strip Set #4 Diagram*. Make 3 Strip Set #4. From strip sets, cut 12 (9½"-wide) #4 segments.

5. Join 2 (2"-wide) light green print strips, 1 (2"-wide) green dot strip, 1 (1½"-wide) blue dot strip, and 1 (4"-wide) light green print strip as shown in *Strip Set #5 Diagram*. Make 2 Strip Set #5. From strip sets, cut 6 (9½"-wide) #5 segments.

6. Join 2 (2"-wide) light blue print strips, 1 (2"-wide) green dot strip, 1 (1½"-wide) blue dot strip, and 1 (4"-wide) light blue print strip as shown in *Strip Set #6 Diagram*. Make 2 Strip Set #6. From strip sets, cut 6 (9½"-wide) #6 segments.

Quilt Assembly

1. Lay out segments as shown in *Quilt Top Assembly Diagram*.

2. Join into rows; join rows to complete quilt top.

Finishing

1. Divide backing into 2 (1¾-yard) lengths. Join panels lengthwise. Seam will run horizontally.

2. Layer backing, batting, and quilt top; baste. Quilt as desired. Quilt shown was machine quilted with an allover design using variegated thread *(Quilting Diagram)*.

3. Join (2¼"-wide) light stripe strips into 1 continuous piece for straight-grain French-fold binding. Add binding to quilt.

Quilting Diagram

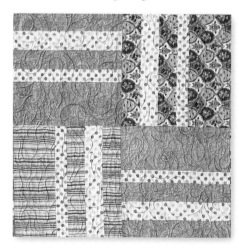

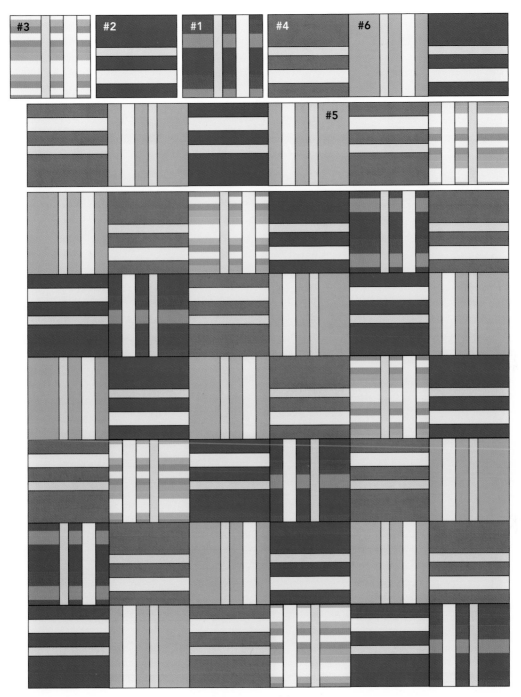

Quilt Top Assembly Diagram

TRIED & TRUE

We used the Full Sun collection by
Willowberry Lane for Maywood Studio
to add rustic charm to this version
of *Sassy Stripes*.

SIZE OPTIONS

	Table Topper (27" × 27")	Twin (63" × 90")	Full (81" x 99")
Blocks	9	70	99
Setting	3 × 3	7 × 10	9 x 11
MATERIALS			
Blue Dot	½ yard	1 yard	1¼ yards
Green Dot	⅝ yard	1⅜ yards	1⅝ yards
Dark Blue Print	¼ yard	1¼ yards	1½ yards
Dark Green Print	¼ yard	1¼ yards	1⅝ yards
Dark Stripe	¼ yard	¾ yard	1 yard
Light Stipe	½ yard	1⅛ yards	1½ yards
Light Blue Print	¼ yard	¾ yard	1 yard
Light Green Print	¼ yard	¾ yard	⅞ yard
Backing Fabric	1 yard	5⅜ yards	7½ yards
Batting	Crib-size	Full-size	Queen-size

Table Topper

Twin Size

Full Size

Jukebox

Designer Cherri House combined big dots, playful flowers, and colorful stripes in this quilt that's as fun to make as it is to display.

Size: 51½" × 72"
Blocks: 6 (12") Pinwheel blocks
6 (12") Box blocks

MATERIALS

⅝ yard each brown dots, cream dots, blue flower, pink flower, green flower, and cream stripe
½ yard red dots
1⅛ yards brown stripe
⅛ yard beige print
2⅛ yards border stripe for borders
3¼ yards backing fabric
Twin-size quilt batting

NOTE: Fabrics in the quilt shown are from the Jitterbug collection by Cosmo Cricket for Andover Fabrics.

Cutting

Measurements include ¼" seam allowances. Border strips are exact length needed. You may want to make them longer to allow for piecing variations.

From each of brown dots and cream dots, cut:

- 1 (12½"-wide) strip. From strip, cut 3 (12½") B squares.
- 1 (6½"-wide) strip. From strip, cut 1 (6½") A square.

From each of blue flower print and pink flower print, cut:

- 1 (6½"-wide) strip. From strip, cut 4 (6½") A squares.
- 1 (3⅞"-wide) strip. From strip, cut 8 (3⅞") squares. Cut squares in half diagonally to make 16 half-square E triangles.
- 2 (3½"-wide) strips. From strips, cut 4 (3½" × 12½") D rectangles and 4 (3½" × 6½") C rectangles.

From green flower print, cut:

- 1 (6½"-wide) strip. From strip, cut 4 (6½") A squares.
- 1 (3⅞"-wide) strip. From strip, cut 8 (3⅞") squares. Cut squares in half diagonally to make 16 half-square E triangles.
- 1 (3½"-wide) strip. From strip, cut 2 (3½" × 12½") D rectangles and 2 (3½" × 6½") C rectangles.

From cream stripe, cut:

- 1 (12½"-wide) strip. From strip, cut 2 (12½") B squares and 1 (6½") A square.
- 2 (3⅞"-wide) strips. From strips, cut 12 (3⅞") squares. Cut squares in half diagonally to make 24 half-square E triangles.

From red dots, cut:

- 1 (12½"-wide) strip. From strip, cut 2 (12½") B squares and 2 (6½") A squares.

From brown stripe, cut:

- 1 (12½"-wide) strip. From strip, cut 2 (12½") B squares and 1 (6½") A square.
- 2 (3⅞"-wide) strips. From strips, cut 12 (3⅞") squares. Cut squares in half diagonally to make 24 half-square E triangles.
- 7 (2¼"-wide) strips for binding.

From beige print, cut:

- 1 (3½"-wide) strip. From strip, cut 2 (3½" × 12½") D rectangles and 2 (3½" × 6½") C rectangles.

From border stripe, cut:

- 2 (2¼"-wide) **lengthwise** strips, centering design in each. From strips, cut 2 (2¼" × 72½") side borders.

Pinwheel Block Assembly

1. Join 1 pink flower print E triangle and 1 cream stripe E triangle as shown in *Triangle-Square Diagrams.* Make 16 pink/cream triangle-squares.

Triangle-Square Diagrams

2. In the same manner, make 16 blue/brown triangle-squares, 8 green/brown triangle-squares, and 8 green/cream triangle-squares.

3. Join 4 pink/cream triangle-squares as shown in *Pinwheel Unit Diagrams.* Make 4 pink Pinwheel Units.

Pinwheel Unit Diagrams

4. Lay out 2 pink Pinwheel Units and 2 pink flower print A squares as shown in *Pinwheel Block Assembly Diagram.* Make 2 pink Pinwheel blocks. Join into rows; join rows to complete 1 Pinwheel block *(Pinwheel Block Diagram).*

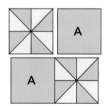 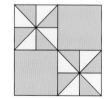

Pinwheel Block Assembly Diagram

Pinwheel Block Diagram

5. In the same manner, make 2 blue Pinwheel blocks and 2 green Pinwheel blocks.

Box Block Assembly

1. Lay out 2 blue flower print C rectangles, 2 blue flower print D rectangles, and 1 brown stripe A square

as shown in *Box Block Assembly Diagram.* Join to complete 1 Box block *(Box Block Diagram).*

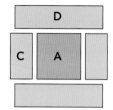 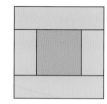

Box Block Assembly Diagram

Box Block Diagram

2. In the same manner, make 5 additional Box blocks using photo on page 57 and *Quilt Top Assembly Diagram* for color reference.

Quilt Assembly

1. Referring to *Quilt Top Assembly Diagram,* lay out blocks and B squares as shown. Join into rows; join rows to complete quilt center.

2. Add borders to sides of quilt.

Finishing

1. Divide backing into 2 (1⅝-yard) lengths. Join panels lengthwise. Seam will run horizontally.

2. Layer backing, batting, and quilt top; baste. Quilt as desired. Quilt shown was quilted with an allover swirl pattern *(Quilting Diagram).*

3. Join 2¼"-wide brown stripe strips into 1 continuous piece for straight-grain French-fold binding. Add binding to quilt.

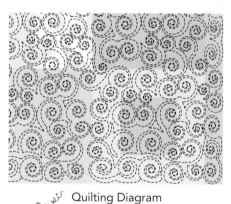

Quilting Diagram

Quilt Top Assembly Diagram

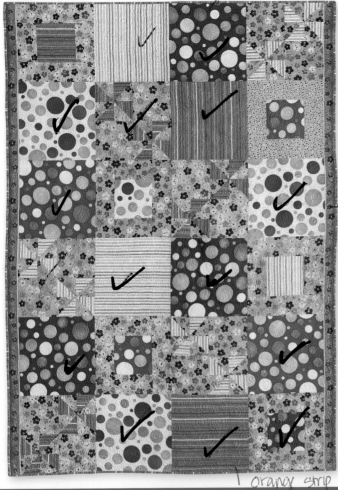

flower

Blue DOT

Orange strip

DESIGNER

Cherri House is a quilt artist and pattern designer who loves scrap and utility quilts. She and her daughter Elizabeth own Cherry House Quilts, selling patterns for contemporary quilts and traditional quilts with a twist.

Contact her at: (281) 852-5011
cherryhousequilts@gmail.com
www.cherryhousequilts.com

WEB EXTRA
Go to www.FonsandPorter.com/jukeboxsizes to download *Quilt Top Assembly Diagrams* for these size options.

SIZE OPTIONS

	Crib (39½" × 48")	Twin (63½" × 84")	Full (75½" × 96")
Pinwheel Blocks	3	9	12
Box Blocks	2	9	12
Setting	3 × 4	5 × 7	6 × 8
MATERIALS			
Red Dot	⅜ yard	⅝ yard	¾ yard
Brown Dot	⅜ yard	¾ yard	1 yard
Cream Dot	⅜ yard	¾ yard	¾ yard
Blue Flower	⅜ yard	1⅛ yards	1⅛ yards
Pink Flower	⅛ yard	½ yard	⅝ yard
Green Flower	⅜ yard	⅝ yard	1 yard
Cream Stripe	⅜ yard	⅞ yard	1¼ yards
Brown Stripe	1 yard	1½ yards	1¾ yards
Beige Print	—	⅛ yard	¾ yard
Border Stripe	1½ yards	2½ yards	2¾ yards
Backing Fabric	2½ yards	5 yards	5¾ yards
Batting	Crib-size	Twin-size	Queen-size

Lizzy's Parade

Choose a group of wild prints and mix them up to make this easy throw. This is a great pattern to showcase themed fabrics for a den or a kid's room.

Size: 67½" × 72"

MATERIALS

2¼ yards white print

⅜ yard each of 12 assorted prints for triangles

⅝ yard each of 5 assorted prints for triangles and sashing

1 yard orange print for triangles, sashing, and binding

4¼ yards backing fabric

Twin-size quilt batting

NOTE: Fabrics in the quilt shown are from the Red Letter Day collection by Lizzy House for Andover Fabrics.

Cutting

Measurements include ¼" seam allowances. Pattern for Triangle is on page 61. Sashing strips are exact length needed. You may want to make them longer to allow for piecing variations.

From white print, cut:

• 9 (8¾"-wide) strips. From strips, cut 86 Triangles.

From each of 18 prints, cut:

• 1 (8¾"-wide) strip. From strip, cut 5 Triangles. **NOTE:** Pay careful attention to orientation of triangle on directional fabrics.

Sew **Smart**™
Point of triangle is trimmed to ensure perfect alignment of fabric triangles.—Marianne

From remainder of each of 3 prints, cut:

• 4 (2"-wide) strips. Piece strips to make 2 (2" × 72½") sashing strips.

From remainder of each of 2 prints, cut:

• 2 (2"-wide) strips. Piece strips to make 1 (2" × 72½") sashing strip.

From remainder of orange print, cut:

• 8 (2¼"-wide) strips for binding.

• 2 (2"-wide) strips. Piece strips to make 1 (2" × 72½") sashing strip.

Row Assembly

1. Join 1 white print triangle and 1 print triangle as shown in *Triangle Unit Diagrams*. Make 86 Triangle Units.

Triangle Unit Diagrams

2. Referring to *Quilt Top Assembly Diagram* page 60, join 10 Triangle Units to complete 1 Row A. Make 5 Row A.

3. In the same manner, join 9 Triangle Units to complete 1 Row B. Make 4 Row B.

4. Trim each Row A to 72½", trimming an equal amount from each end.

Sew **Smart**™
The measurement of each row should be 72½" including seam allowances. —Liz

Quilt Assembly

1. Lay out rows and sashing strips as shown in *Quilt Top Assembly Diagram* on page 60.

2. Join rows and strips to complete quilt top.

Quilt Top Assembly Diagram

Finishing

1. Divide backing fabric into 2 (2⅛-yard) lengths. Cut 1 piece in half lengthwise to make 2 narrow panels. Join 1 narrow panel to each side of wider panel; press seam allowances toward narrow panels.

2. Layer backing, batting, and quilt top; baste. Quilt as desired. Quilt shown was quilted ⅛" from edge of each white triangle and each sashing strip *(Quilting Diagram)*.

3. Join 2¼"-wide orange print strips into 1 continuous piece for straight-grain French-fold binding. Add binding to quilt.

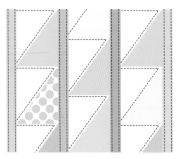

Quilting Diagram

WEB EXTRA

Go to www.FonsandPorter.com/lizzysparadesizes to download size options and *Quilt Top Assembly Diagrams* for additional sizes.

Triangle

DESIGNER

Cherri House made her first quilt at the age of twelve, and now owns a pattern design business with her daughter, Lizzy House. Lizzy designed the fabric in this quilt for Andover.

Contact her at:

cherryhousequilts@gmail.com

www.cherryhousequilts.com ✳

TRIED & TRUE

Red and black prints from the Always And Forever collection by Alex Anderson for P&B Textiles provide perfect contrast in our sample.

QUILT BY **Jodie Davis**.

MACHINE QUILTED BY **Mavis Rosbach**.

Primarily Stars

Jodie Davis of QNNtv designed this scrappy star. At first glance you see red stars, but careful color placement makes a secondary blue star pattern appear.

Size: 63" × 81"

Blocks: 12 (18") Star blocks

MATERIALS

12 fat eighths★★ assorted green prints

8 fat quarters★ assorted red prints

6 fat eighths★★ assorted blue prints

6 fat quarters★ assorted yellow prints

9 fat quarters★ assorted tan prints

½ yard blue print for inner border

¾ yard red print for binding

Fons & Porter Half & Quarter Ruler (optional)

5 yards backing fabric

Twin-size quilt batting

★fat quarter = 18" × 20"

★★fat eighth = 9" × 20"

Cutting

Measurements include ¼" seam allowances. Border strips are exact length needed. You may want to make them longer to allow for piecing variations.

WEB EXTRA

To cut triangles for triangle-squares using the Fons & Porter Half & Quarter Ruler, refer to *Sew Easy: Cutting Half-Square Triangles* on page 39. If you are not using the Fons & Porter Half & Quarter Ruler, use the cutting **NOTE** instructions given here.

From each green print fat eighth, cut:

• 1 (6½"-wide) strip. From strip, cut 1 (6½") A square.

From red print fat quarters, cut a total of:

• 19 (3½"-wide) strips. From strips, cut 92 (3½") B squares.

• 12 (3½"-wide) strips. From strips, cut 96 half-square D triangles.

NOTE: If NOT using the Fons & Porter Half & Quarter Ruler to cut the D triangles, cut 12 (3⅞"-wide) strips. From strips, cut 48 (3⅞") squares. Cut squares in half diagonally to make 96 half-square D triangles.

From each blue print fat eighth, cut:

• 2 (3½"-wide) strips. From strips, cut 16 half-square D triangles.

NOTE: If NOT using the Fons & Porter Half & Quarter Ruler to cut the D triangles, cut 2 (3⅞"-wide) strips. From strips, cut 8 (3⅞") squares. Cut squares in half diagonally to make 16 half-square D triangles.

From each yellow print fat quarter, cut:

• 4 (3½"-wide) strips. From strips, cut 32 half-square D triangles.

NOTE: If NOT using the Fons & Porter Half & Quarter Ruler to cut the D triangles, cut 4 (3⅞"-wide) strips. From strips, cut 16 (3⅞") squares. Cut squares in half diagonally to make 32 half-square D triangles.

From tan print fat quarters, cut a total of:

• 10 (6½"-wide) strips. From strips, cut 48 (6½" × 3½") C rectangles.

• 20 (3½"-wide) strips. From strips, cut 96 (3½") B squares.

From blue print, cut:

• 7 (2"-wide) strips. Piece strips to make 2 (2" × 72½") side inner borders and 2 (2" × 57½") top and bottom inner borders.

From red print, cut:

• 8 (2¼"-wide) strips for binding.

Block Assembly

1. Join 1 yellow print D triangle and 1 blue print D triangle as shown in *Triangle-Square Diagrams*. Make 96 yellow/blue triangle-squares.

Triangle-Square Diagrams

2. In the same manner, make 96 yellow/red triangle-squares using yellow print and red print D triangles.

3. Lay out 8 tan print B squares, 4 tan print C rectangles, 8 assorted yellow/blue triangle-squares, 8 assorted yellow/red triangle-squares, and 1 green print A square as shown in *Block Assembly Diagram*. Join into rows; join rows to complete 1 Star block *(Block Diagram)*. Make 12 blocks.

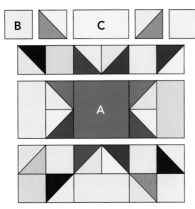

Block Assembly Diagram

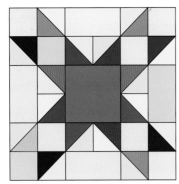

Block Diagram

Quilt Top Assembly Diagram

Quilt Assembly

1. Lay out blocks as shown in *Quilt Top Assembly Diagram*. Join into rows; join rows to complete quilt center.

2. Add blue print side inner borders to quilt center. Add top and bottom inner borders to quilt.

3. Join 25 assorted red print B squares to make 1 pieced side outer border. Make 2 pieced side outer borders. Add borders to quilt.

4. Join 21 assorted red print B squares to make pieced top outer border. Repeat for pieced bottom outer border. Add borders to quilt.

Finishing

1. Divide backing into 2 (2½-yard) lengths. Cut 1 piece in half lengthwise to make 2 narrow panels. Join 1 narrow panel to each side of wider panel; press seam allowances toward narrow panels.

2. Layer backing, batting, and quilt top; baste. Quilt as desired. Quilt shown was quilted with stars and swirls *(Quilting Diagram)*.

3. Join 2¼"-wide red print strips into 1 continuous piece for straight-grain French-fold binding. Add binding to quilt.

Quilting Diagram

TRIED & TRUE

Assorted blue-and-white prints are perfect for a two-color quilt. Fabrics shown are from the Cambridge Square collection by Northcott.

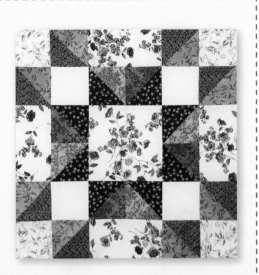

SIZE OPTIONS

	Crib (45" × 45")	Full (81" × 99")	Queen (99" × 117")
Blocks	4	20	30
Setting	2 × 2	4 × 5	5 × 6
MATERIALS			
Green Prints	4 fat eighths	5 fat quarters	8 fat quarters
Red Prints	4 fat quarters	12 fat quarters	15 fat quarters
Blue Prints	2 fat eighths	5 fat quarters	8 fat quarters
Yellow Prints	2 fat quarters	10 fat quarters	15 fat quarters
Tan Prints	4 fat quarters	14 fat quarters	20 fat quarters
Blue Print	⅜ yard	⅝ yard	¾ yard
Red Print	½ yard	¾ yard	1 yard
Backing Fabric	1½ yards	7½ yards	9 yards
Batting	Twin-size	Queen-size	King-size

 WEB EXTRA

Go to www.FonsandPorter.com/primarilysizes to download *Quilt Top Assembly Diagrams* for these size options.

DESIGNER

Jodie Davis loves paper piecing, but admits that not all quilts call for this technique. Once in awhile she likes to practice her traditional piecing skills while making scrappy stash-busting quilts. You'll find Jodie on QNNtv.com as host of *Quilt Out Loud* and *Quilt It! the Longarm Quilting Show.*

Contact her at: www.QNNtv.com ✳

QUILT DESIGNED AND MADE BY **Sarah Maxwell and Dolores Smith.**
MACHINE QUILTED BY **Connie Gresham.**

Inkwell

Designers Sarah Maxwell and Dolores Smith made this quilt with simple blocks in bold black-and-tan prints. They used a complementary toile for the setting triangles.

Size: 72¾" × 85½"
Blocks: 30 (9") Shoo Fly blocks

MATERIALS

½ yard each of 6 assorted light
  prints in tan and cream
6 fat quarters★ assorted black prints
4¼ yards black toile
5¼ yards backing fabric
Full-size quilt batting
★fat quarter = 18" × 20"

NOTE: Fabrics in the quilt shown are from the Inkwell and Classic Toile collections by Judie Rothermel for Marcus Fabrics.

Cutting

Measurements include ¼" seam allowances. Border strips are exact length needed. You may want to make them longer to allow for piecing variations.

From each light print, cut:

- 2 (4⅝"-wide) strips. From strips, cut 10 (4⅝") squares. Cut squares in half diagonally to make 20 half-square A triangles.
- 1 (4¼"-wide) strip. From strip, cut 20 (4¼" × 2") C rectangles.

From each black print fat quarter, cut:

- 3 (4⅝"-wide) strips. From strips, cut 10 (4⅝") squares. Cut squares in half diagonally to make 20 half-square A triangles.
- 1 (2"-wide) strip. From strip, cut 5 (2") B squares.

From black toile, cut:

- 3 (14"-wide) strips. From strips, cut 5 (14") squares and 2 (7¼") squares. Cut 14" squares in half diagonally in both directions to make 20 side setting triangles (2 are extra). Cut 7¼" squares in half diagonally to make 4 corner setting triangles.
- 5 (9½"-wide) strips. From strips, cut 20 (9½") D squares.
- 8 (5"-wide) strips. Piece strips to make 2 (5" × 77") side borders and 2 (5" × 73¼") top and bottom borders.
- 9 (2¼"-wide) strips for binding.

Block Assembly

1. Join 1 black print A triangle and 1 light print A triangle as shown in *Triangle-Square Diagrams.* Make 30 sets of 4 matching triangle-squares.

Triangle-Square Diagrams

2. Lay out 1 set of triangle squares, 1 black print B square, and 4 matching light print C rectangles as shown in *Block Assembly Diagram.* Join into rows; join rows to complete 1 Shoo Fly block *(Block Diagram).* Make 30 blocks.

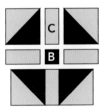

Block Assembly Diagram

Block Diagram

Quilt Assembly

1. Lay out blocks, black toile D squares, and setting triangles as shown in *Quilt Top Assembly Diagram*. Join into diagonal rows; join rows to complete quilt center.

2. Add side borders to quilt center. Add top and bottom borders to quilt.

Finishing

1. Divide backing into 2 (2⅝-yard) lengths. Cut 1 piece in half lengthwise to make 2 narrow panels. Join 1 narrow panel to each side of wider panel; press seam allowances toward narrow panels.

2. Layer backing, batting, and quilt top; baste. Quilt as desired. Quilt shown was quilted with assorted feather designs *(Quilting Diagram)*.

3. Join 2¼"-wide black toile strips into 1 continuous piece for straight-grain French-fold binding. Add binding to quilt.

Quilt Top Assembly Diagram

Quilting Diagram

SIZE OPTIONS

	Throw (60" × 72¾")	Queen (85½" × 98¼")
Blocks	20	42
Setting	4 × 5	6 × 7
MATERIALS		
6 Assorted Light Prints	1 fat quarter each	⅝ yard each
6 Assorted Black Prints	1 fat quarter each	⅜ yard each
Black Toile	3½ yards	5¾ yards
Backing Fabric	3¾ yards	7¾ yards
Batting	Twin-size	Queen-size

DESIGNERS

Sarah Maxwell and Dolores Smith, owners of Homestead Hearth™ pattern company, have a passion for creating original patterns using many prints from their stash or from a single fabric line.

Contact them at:

info@homesteadhearth.com • www.homesteadhearth.com ✳

TRIED & TRUE

Make a fresh, summery table runner with fabrics from the Chloe line by Janet Broxon for P&B Textiles.

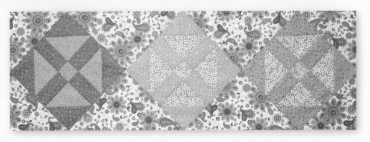

QUILT BY **Jean Ann Wright**.
MACHINE QUILTED BY **Jan Crandall**.

Sound Waves

Jean Ann Wright used raw edge appliqué to create rhythm in her lively blocks. Try our cutting and piecing techniques on page 75 to make the curvy nine patch units.

Size: 59" × 59"
Blocks: 9 (15") blocks

MATERIALS

- 6 fat quarters★ assorted prints in blue, green, rust, and cream for blocks
- ⅞ yard dark blue print for blocks and binding
- 1 yard light blue print for blocks and inner border
- 1 yard green print for blocks and inner border
- 1⅛ yards black print #1 for block backgrounds
- 1⅛ yards black print #2 for outer border
- 3¾ yards backing fabric
- Twin-size quilt batting
- ★fat quarter = 18" × 20"

NOTE: Fabrics in the quilt shown are from the All That Jazz collection by Windham Fabrics.

Cutting

Measurements include ¼" seam allowances. Border strips are exact length needed. You may want to make them longer to allow for piecing variations.

From each fat quarter, cut:
- 1 (11"-wide) strip. From strip, cut 1 (11") square.

From dark blue print, cut:
- 1 (11"-wide) strip. From strip, cut 1 (11") square.
- 7 (2¼"-wide) strips for binding.

From light blue print, cut:
- 1 (11"-wide) strip. From strip, cut 1 (11") square.
- 11 (2"-wide) strips. From strips, cut 14 (2" × 15½") C rectangles and 10 (2" × 12½") B rectangles.

From green print, cut:
- 1 (11"-wide) strip. From strip, cut 1 (11") square.
- 11 (2"-wide) strips. From strips, cut 4 (2" × 17") D rectangles, 12 (2" × 15½") C rectangles and 8 (2" × 12½") B rectangles.

From black print #1, cut:

- 3 (12½"-wide) strips. From strips, cut 9 (12½") A squares.

From black print #2, cut:

- 6 (6"-wide) strips. Piece strips to make 2 (6" × 59½") top and bottom borders and 2 (6" × 48½") side borders.

Block Assembly

1. Referring to *Sew Easy: Making Curvy Nine Patch Units* on page 75, cut pieces for blocks. Make 9 Curvy Nine Patch Units.

2. Trim Nine Patch Units to 9½" square, using pinking shears or scalloped rotary cutter blade.

3. Join 1 black print #1 A square, 2 light blue print B rectangles, and 2 light blue print C rectangles as shown in *Block Background Diagrams*. Make 5 blue block backgrounds. In the same manner, make 4 green block backgrounds using 1 black print #1 A square, 2 green print B rectangles, and 2 green print C rectangles for each.

4. Referring to quilt photo on page 74, arrange 1 Nine Patch Unit atop 1 block background. Stitch ¼" inside edges of Nine Patch Unit to complete 1 block. Make 9 blocks.

NOTE: Blocks with blue background are tilted to the right; blocks with green background are tilted to the left.

Inner Border Assembly

1. Join 1 blue print C rectangle and 2 green print C rectangles to make 1 side inner border as shown in *Quilt Top Assembly Diagram*. Make 2 side inner borders.

2. Join 1 blue print C rectangle and 2 green print D rectangles to make top inner border. Repeat for bottom inner border.

Quilt Assembly

1. Lay out blocks as shown in *Quilt Top Assembly Diagram*. Join into rows; join rows to complete quilt center.

2. Add side inner borders to quilt center. Add top and bottom inner borders to quilt.

3. Add black print #2 side outer borders to quilt center. Add top and bottom outer borders to quilt.

Finishing

1. Divide backing into 2 (1⅞-yard) lengths. Cut 1 piece in half lengthwise to make 2 narrow panels. Join 1 narrow panel to each side of wider panel; press seam allowances toward narrow panels.

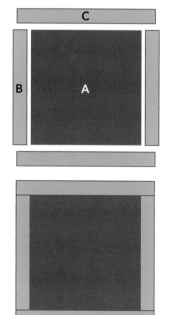

Block Background Diagrams

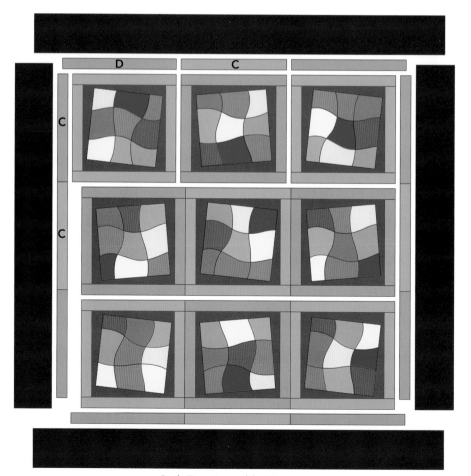

Quilt Top Assembly Diagram

2. Layer backing, batting, and quilt top; baste. Quilt as desired. Quilt shown was quilted with an allover rectangle pattern *(Quilting Diagram)*.

3. Join 2¼"-wide dark blue print strips into 1 continuous piece for straight-grain French-fold binding. Add binding to quilt.

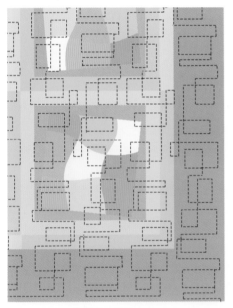

Quilting Diagram

TRIED & TRUE

Use soft colors such as these from the Mama's Cottons 2 collection by Connecting Threads for a look reminiscent of grandma's aprons.

SIZE OPTIONS

	Twin (74" × 89")	Full/Queen (89" × 104")	King (104" × 104")
Blocks	20	30	36
Setting	4 × 5	5 × 6	6 × 6

MATERIALS

Assorted Prints	21 fat quarters	27 fat quarters	27 fat quarters
Dark Blue Print	1 yard	1⅛ yards	1⅛ yards
Light Blue Print	1⅜ yards	1⅝ yards	2⅛ yards
Green Print	1⅜ yards	1⅝ yards	2⅛ yards
Black Print #1	2⅝ yards	3⅝ yards	4½ yards
Black Print #2	1½ yards	1⅞ yards	2 yards
Backing Fabric	5½ yards	8 yards	9¼ yards
Batting	Full-size	Queen-size	King-size

WEB EXTRA

Go to www.FonsandPorter.com/soundwavessizes to download *Quilt Top Assembly Diagrams* for these size options.

DESIGNER

Jean Ann Wright has been designing quilts for more than twenty years. Her favorites are made from traditional blocks laid out in new ways. Jean Ann says she never runs out of ideas!

Contact her at: jeanannquilts.com ✳

Sew Easy™

Making Curvy Nine Patch Units

Use these quick and easy techniques to cut and sew
Curvy Nine Patch Units for *Sound Waves* on page 70.

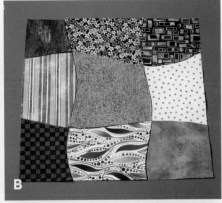

1. Stack 9 (11") squares, right sides up, aligning all edges. Using large rotary cutter, make 2 curved horizontal cuts and 2 curved vertical cuts *(Photo A)*. Number the stacks of pieces from 1–9.

Sew **Smart**™

To make cutting through 9 layers of fabric easier, use a large (60mm) rotary cutter and make gentle curves for easier piecing. —Liz

2. Move top piece from stack #2 to bottom of stack. Move top 2 pieces from stack #3 to bottom of stack. Continue rearranging the pieces in this manner, moving 1 additional piece to bottom of each successive stack.

3. Lay out the top piece from each stack as shown in *Photo B*.

4. Place first 2 pieces together, right sides facing. Pin top corner *(Photo C)*.

5. Sew pieces together, aligning edges as you go *(Photo D)*. Join pieces for each row in the same manner.

Sew **Smart**™

Press seam allowances in top and bottom rows toward the right. Press seam allowances in center row toward the left. —Marianne

6. Pin top and center rows together at beginning and at each seam *(Photo E)*. Stitch, aligning edges as you go. Add bottom row to top 2 rows to complete Curvy Nine Patch Unit *(Photo F)*.

Dancing Squares

In this quilt designed by Nancy Mahoney, the border blocks are turned to make the brown squares in the border dance around the quilt.

Size: 62" × 72"
Blocks: 30 (10") blocks

MATERIALS

1⅝ yards brown print for blocks, inner border, and binding
¾ yard green print for blocks
⅝ yard blue print for blocks
⅝ yard orange print for blocks
1¾ yards cream print #1 for blocks and outer border
⅝ yard cream print #2 for blocks
⅝ yard cream print #3 for blocks
⅜ yard cream print #4 for blocks
4 yards backing fabric
Twin-size quilt batting

NOTE: Fabrics in the quilt shown are from the Pop Parade 2 collection by P&B Textiles.

Cutting

Measurements include ¼" seam allowances. Border strips are exact length needed. You may want to make them longer to allow for piecing variations.

From brown print, cut:
- 3 (2⅝"-wide) strips for strip sets.
- 8 (2¼"-wide) strips for binding.
- 18 (1½"-wide) strips. From 11 strips, cut 30 (1½" × 7½") D rectangles and 30 (1½" × 5½") C rectangles. Piece remaining strips to make 2 (1½" × 60½") side inner borders and 2 (1½" × 52½") top and bottom inner borders.

From green print, cut:
- 3 (4"-wide) strips. From strips, cut 30 (4") B squares.
- 3 (3"-wide) strips for strip sets.

From blue print, cut:
- 8 (2"-wide) strips. From strips, cut 30 (2" × 5½") F rectangles and 30 (2" × 4") E rectangles.

From orange print, cut:
- 8 (2"-wide) strips. From strips, cut 30 (2" × 5½") F rectangles and 30 (2" × 4") E rectangles.

From cream print #1, cut:
- 7 (5½"-wide) strips. From strips, cut 15 (5½") A squares, 42 (5½" × 2⅝") H rectangles, 4 (5½" × 2") J rectangles, 18 (5½" × 1½") I rectangles, 16 (5½" × 1¼") K rectangles, and 4 (5½" × 1") L rectangles.

- 3 (2⅝"-wide) strips for strip sets.
- 9 (1¼"-wide) strips. From 6 strips, cut 42 (1¼" × 5½") G rectangles. Remaining strips are for strip sets.

From cream print #2, cut:
- 8 (2"-wide) strips. From strips, cut 30 (2" × 5½") F rectangles and 30 (2" × 4") E rectangles.

From cream print #3, cut:
- 3 (5½"-wide) strips. From strips, cut 15 (5½") A squares.

From cream print #4, cut:
- 3 (3"-wide) strips for strip sets.

Block 1 Assembly

1. Join 1 green print strip and 1 cream print #4 strip as shown in *Strip Set #1 Diagram*. Make 3 Strip Set #1. From strip sets, cut 30 (3"-wide) #1 segments.

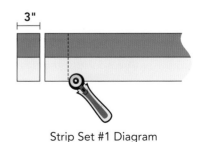

Strip Set #1 Diagram

2. Join 2 #1 segments as shown in *Four Patch Unit Diagrams*. Make 15 Four Patch Units.

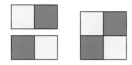

Four Patch Unit Diagrams

3. Lay out 1 Four Patch Unit, 2 brown print C rectangles, and 2 brown print D rectangles as shown in *Center Unit Diagrams*. Join to complete 1 Center Unit. Make 15 Center Units.

Center Unit Diagrams

4. Lay out 1 Center Unit, 2 blue print E rectangles, 2 cream print #2 E rectangles, 2 blue print F rectangles, and 2 cream print #2 F rectangles as shown in *Block 1 Assembly Diagram*. Join to complete 1 Block 1 *(Block 1 Diagram)*. Make 15 Block 1.

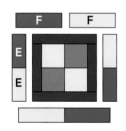

Block 1 Assembly Diagram

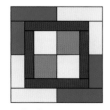

Block 1 Diagram

Block 2 Assembly

1. Lay out 1 green print B square, 1 orange print E rectangle, and 1 orange print F rectangle as shown in *Corner Unit Diagrams*. Join to complete 1 Corner Unit. Make 30 Corner Units.

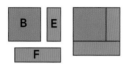

Corner Unit Diagrams

2. Lay out 2 Corner Units, 1 cream print #1 A square, and 1 cream print #3 A square as shown in *Block 2 Assembly Diagram*. Join to complete 1 Block 2 *(Block 2 Diagram)*. Make 15 Block 2.

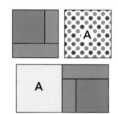

Block 2 Assembly Diagram

Block 2 Diagram

Border Assembly

1. Join 1 (2⅝"-wide) cream print #1 strip, 1 (2⅝"-wide) brown print strip, and 1 (1¼"-wide) cream print #1 strip as shown in *Strip Set #2 Diagram*. Make 3 Strip Set #2. From strip sets, cut 42 (2⅝"-wide) #2 segments.

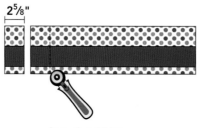

Strip Set #2 Diagram

2. Lay out 1 #2 segment, 1 cream print #1 G rectangle, and 1 cream print #1 H rectangle as shown in *Border Block Assembly Diagram*. Join to complete 1 border block *(Border Block Diagram)*. Make 42 border blocks.

Border Block Assembly Diagram

Border Block Diagram

3. Lay out 10 border blocks, 9 cream print #1 I rectangles, and 2 cream print #1 J rectangles as shown in *Quilt Top Assembly Diagram*. Join to make 1 side outer border. Make 2 side outer borders.

> ### Sew **Smart**™
> Turn the border blocks as shown to make the brown squares in the border dance around the quilt. — Marianne

4. In the same manner, join 11 border blocks, 8 cream print #1 K rectangles, and 2 cream print #1 L rectangles to make top outer border. Repeat for bottom outer border.

Quilt Assembly

1. Lay out blocks as shown in *Quilt Top Assembly Diagram*. Join into rows; join rows to complete quilt center.

2. Add brown print side inner borders to quilt center. Add brown print top and bottom inner borders to quilt.

3. Repeat for pieced outer borders.

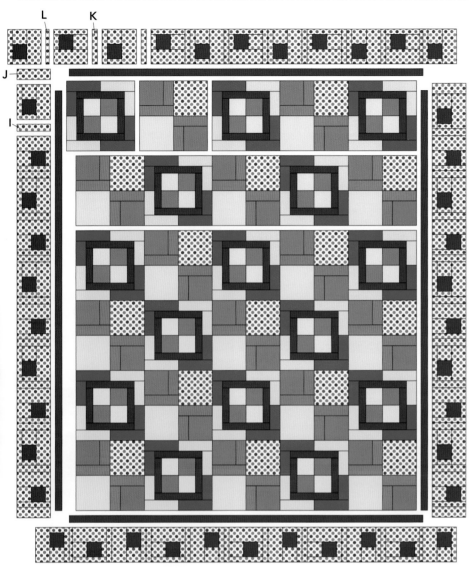

Quilt Top Assembly Diagram

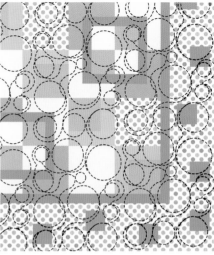

Quilting Diagram

DESIGNER

A prolific quiltmaker and author of nine books, Nancy Mahoney is also a teacher and fabric designer.

She enjoys making traditional quilts using new techniques that make quiltmaking easy and fun.

Contact her at:

www.nancymahoney.com ✳

Finishing

1. Divide backing into 2 (2-yard) lengths. Join panels lengthwise. Seam will run horizontally.

2. Layer backing, batting, and quilt top; baste. Quilt as desired. Quilt shown was quilted with an allover circle design *(Quilting Diagram)*.

3. Join 2¼"-wide brown print strips into 1 continuous piece for straight-grain French-fold binding. Add binding to quilt.

TRIED & TRUE

We created elegant blocks using fabrics from the Samsara collection by Benartex.

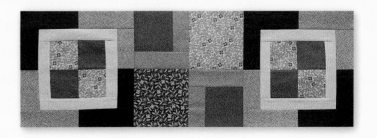

Tiramisu

As you snuggle up under this quilt on a cold winter day,
the rich colors will remind you of mocha and cream.

Size: 49" × 63"

Blocks: 63 (7") Courthouse Steps Log Cabin blocks

MATERIALS

11 fat quarters★ assorted brown
    batiks
½ yard brown batik for binding
2¼ yards cream batik
3¼ yards backing fabric
Twin-size quilt batting
★fat quarter = 18" × 20"

Cutting

Measurements include ¼" seam allowances.

From each brown fat quarter, cut:

- 10 (1½"-wide) strips. From strips, cut:
  - 6 (1½" × 7½") #6 rectangles.
  - 6 (1½" × 5½") #5 rectangles.
  - 6 (1½" × 5½") #4 rectangles.
  - 6 (1½" × 3½") #3 rectangles.
  - 6 (1½" × 3½") #2 rectangles.
  - 6 (1½" × 1½") #1 squares.
  - 3 (1½") center squares.

From brown batik, cut:

- 6 (2¼"-wide) strips for binding.

From cream batik, cut:

- 47 (1½"-wide) strips. From strips, cut:
  - 62 (1½" × 7½") #6 rectangles.
  - 62 (1½" × 5½") #5 rectangles.
  - 64 (1½" × 5½") #4 rectangles.
  - 64 (1½" × 3½") #3 rectangles.
  - 62 (1½" × 3½") #2 rectangles.
  - 62 (1½" × 1½") #1 squares.
  - 32 (1½" × 1½") center squares.

Block Assembly

1. Choose one matching set of 2 each brown batik rectangles #1, #2, #5, and #6, and 1 set of 2 each cream batik rectangles #3 and #4, and 1 cream center square.

2. Lay out pieces as shown in *Brown Block Diagram*.

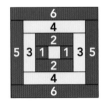

Brown Block Diagram

3. Join pieces in numerical order to complete 1 brown block. Make 32 brown blocks.

4. In a similar manner, make 1 cream block using matching cream batik rectangles #1, #2, #5, and #6, and matching brown batik rectangles #3, #4 and center square *(Cream Block Diagram)*. Make 31 cream blocks.

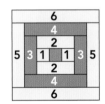

Cream Block Diagram

Quilt Assembly

1. Lay out blocks as shown in *Quilt Top Assembly Diagram*.

2. Join blocks into rows; join rows to complete quilt top.

Finishing

1. Divide backing into 2 (1⅝-yard) lengths. Join panels lengthwise. Seam will run horizontally.

2. Layer backing, batting, and quilt top; baste. Quilt as desired. Quilt shown was quilted with straight lines intersecting the centers of cream blocks and parallel diamonds in brown blocks *(Quilting Diagram)*.

3. Join 2¼"-wide brown batik strips into 1 continuous piece for straight-grain French-fold binding. Add binding to quilt.

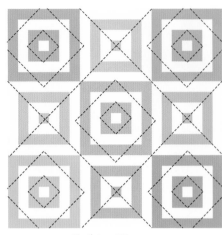

Quilting Diagram

TRIED & TRUE

We combined bright geometric prints in shades of blue and green to make this contemporary version. Fabrics shown are from the Pop Parade collection by Metro for P&B ✳

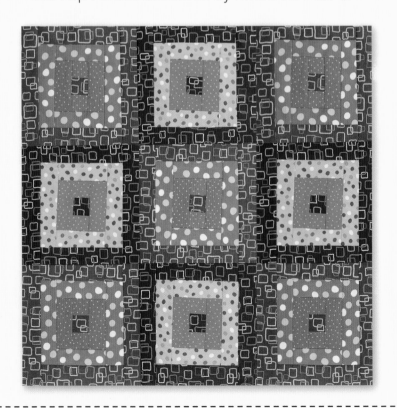

Quilt Top Assembly Diagram

SIZE OPTIONS

	Twin (70" × 84")	Full (84" × 91")	Queen (98" × 105")
Setting	10 × 12 blocks	12 × 13 blocks	14 × 15 blocks
Brown Blocks	60	85	105
Cream Blocks	60	84	105

MATERIALS

Assorted brown batiks	20 fat quarters★	29 fat quarters★	35 fat quarters★
Cream batik	4 yards	5⅜ yards	6¾ yards
Brown batik	¾ yard	⅞ yard	1 yard
Backing Fabric	5 yards	7½ yards	9 yards
Batting	Full-size	Queen-size	King-size

★fat quarter = 18" × 20"

Twin Size

Full Size

Queen Size

Blocks in a Box

The patchwork blocks for this quilt are super simple. Make it in neutral prints with red accents as the one shown here, or choose colors to fit a specific room decor.

Size: 90" × 97½"
Blocks: 156 (7½") blocks

MATERIALS

2 yards red print for blocks and
  binding
¾ yard each of 12 assorted cream
  prints
8¼ yards backing fabric
King-size quilt batting

Cutting

Measurements include ¼" seam allowances.

From red print, cut:

• 12 (3"-wide) strips for strip sets.
• 10 (2¼"-wide) strips for binding.

From each cream print, cut:

• 2 (8"-wide) strips. From each strip, cut 13 (8" × 3") rectangles.
• 2 (3"-wide) strips for strip sets.

Block Assembly

1. Join 2 matching cream print strips and 1 red print strip as shown in *Strip Set Diagram*. Make 12 strip sets. From each strip set, cut 13 (3"-wide) segments.

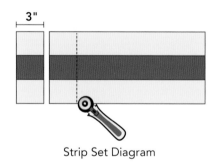

3"

Strip Set Diagram

2. Referring to *Block Assembly Diagram*, join 2 matching cream print rectangles and 1 strip set segment to complete 1 block (*Block Diagram*). Make 156 blocks.

Block Assembly
Diagram

Block Diagram

Quilt Assembly

1. Lay out blocks as shown in *Quilt Top Assembly Diagram* on page 88.

2. Join into rows; join rows to complete quilt top.

> ### Sew **Smart**™
> Rotate blocks as shown in *Quilt Top Assembly Diagram* on page 88 to prevent bulky seams. —Marianne

Finishing

1. Divide backing fabric into (2¾-yard) lengths. Join pieces lengthwise. Seams will run horizontally.

2. Layer backing, batting, and quilt top; baste. Quilt as desired. Quilt shown was quilted with an allover pattern (*Quilting Diagram*).

3. Join 2¼"-wide red print strips into 1 continuous piece for straight-grain French-fold binding. Add binding to quilt.

Quilting Diagram

TRIED & TRUE

Get a country look in reds and blues with fabrics from the Farmhouse West collection by LB Krueger for Windham Fabrics.

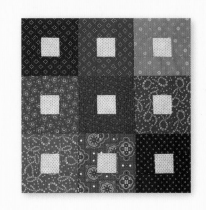

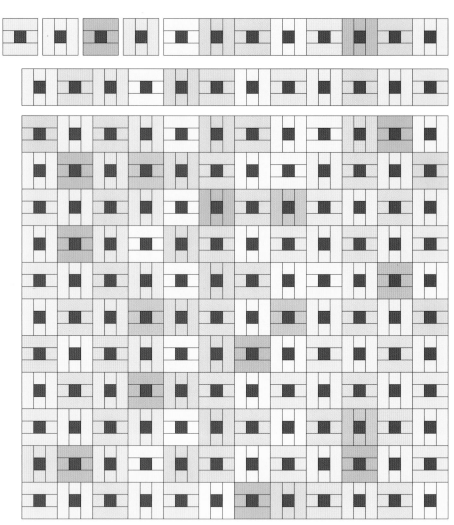

Quilt Top Assembly Diagram

SIZE OPTIONS

	Crib (37½" × 45")	Twin (67½" × 82½")	Full (82½" × 90")
Blocks	30	99	132
Setting	5 × 6	9 × 11	11 × 12
MATERIALS			
Red print	⅝ yard	1⅜ yards	1¾ yards
Cream prints	¾ yard each of 3 prints	¾ yard each of 8 prints	¾ yard each of 11 prints
Backing Fabric	1½ yards	7½ yards	9½ yards
Batting	Crib-size	Twin-size	Queen-size

 WEB EXTRA

Go to www.FonsandPorter.com/blockssizes to download *Quilt Top Assembly Diagrams* for these size options.

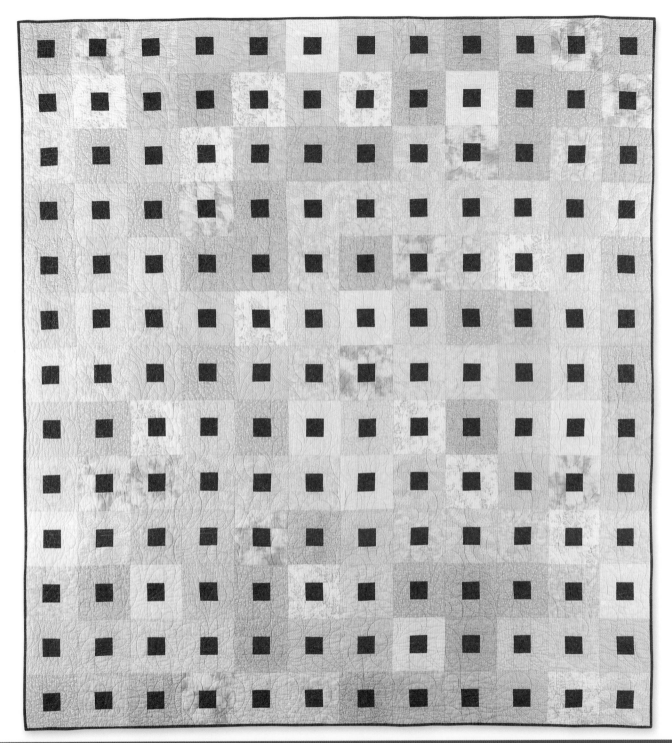

DESIGNER

Author of many pattern and design books, Judy Hopkins grew up in a family of quilters. Making a wedding quilt for her daughter about 25 years ago got her seriously interested in making more. Judy lives in the magnificent state of Alaska with her husband, Bill, who, fortunately for an avid quilter like Judy, loves to cook!

Contact her at: j5hopkins@aol.com ✳

Symphony Hall

Designers Anne Gallo and Susan Raban used Gerald Roy's graphic interpretation of music to make this simple, yet elegant quilt.

Size: 41" × 41"

MATERIALS

⅝ yard medium orange print

⅜ yard white print

4 (6") squares assorted gold prints

2 fat eighths★ assorted light blue prints

4 fat eighths★ assorted medium blue prints

4 fat quarters★★ assorted dark orange prints

5 fat eighths★ assorted green prints

8 fat eighths★ assorted prints in dark blue, purple, tan, and red

2½ yards backing fabric

Crib-size quilt batting

★fat eighth = 9" × 20"

★★fat quarter = 18" × 20"

NOTE: Fabrics in the quilt shown are from the Graphic Rhythms collection by Gerald Roy for Windham Fabrics.

Cutting

Measurements include ¼" seam allowances.

From medium orange print, cut:

- 3 (3½"-wide) strips. From strips, cut 24 (3½") B squares.
- 1 (5½") A square.

From white print, cut:

- 3 (3½"-wide) strips. From strips, cut 60 (3½" × 1½") D rectangles.

From each gold print, cut:

- 1 (3½" × 5½") C rectangle.

From each light blue print, cut:

- 2 (3½"-wide) strips. From strips, cut 4 (3½" × 5½") C rectangles.

From each medium blue print, cut:

- 1 (3½"-wide) strip. From strip, cut 3 (3½" × 5½") C rectangles.

From each dark orange print, cut:

- 1 (5½"-wide) strip. From strip, cut 4 (5½" × 3½") C rectangles.
- 3 (2¼"-wide) strips for binding.

From each green print, cut:

- 1 (5½"-wide) strip. From strip, cut 4 (5½" × 3½") C rectangles.

From each assorted print fat eighth, cut:

- 1 (3½"-wide) strip. From strip, cut 3 (3½" × 5½") C rectangles.

Center Assembly

1. Lay out medium orange print A square, 4 medium orange print B squares, and 4 gold print C rectangles as shown in *Center Assembly Diagram*.

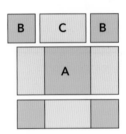

Center Assembly Diagram

2. Join into rows; join rows to complete quilt center (*Center Diagram*).

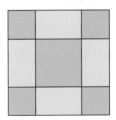

Center Diagram

Side Unit Assembly

1. Referring to *Quilt Top Assembly Diagram*, join 2 light blue print C rectangles and 1 white print D rectangle to make 1 Unit 1. Make 4 Unit 1.

2. Join 3 medium blue print C rectangles and 2 white print D rectangles to make 1 Unit 2. Make 4 Unit 2.

3. Join 4 dark orange print C rectangles and 3 white print D rectangles to make 1 Unit 3. Make 4 Unit 3.

4. Join 5 green print C rectangles and 4 white print D rectangles to make 1 Unit 4. Make 4 Unit 4.

5. Join 6 dark blue, purple, tan, and red print C rectangles and 5 white print D rectangles to make 1 Unit 5. Make 4 Unit 5.

Quilt Assembly

1. Lay out center, Units 1–5, and medium orange B squares as shown in *Quilt Top Assembly Diagram*.

2. Add 1 Unit 1 to each side of center.

3. Add 1 medium orange B square to each end of 2 remaining Unit 1. Add to top and bottom of quilt.

4. Repeat steps #2 and #3 for Unit 2–Unit 5.

Finishing

1. Divide backing into 2 (1¼-yard) lengths. Cut 1 piece in half lengthwise to make 2 narrow panels. Join 1 narrow panel to wider panel. Remaining panel is extra and can be used to make a hanging sleeve.

2. Layer backing, batting, and quilt top; baste. Quilt as desired. Quilt shown was quilted with continuous loops (*Quilting Diagram*).

3. Join 2¼"-wide assorted dark orange print strips into 1 continuous piece for straight-grain French-fold binding. Add binding to quilt.

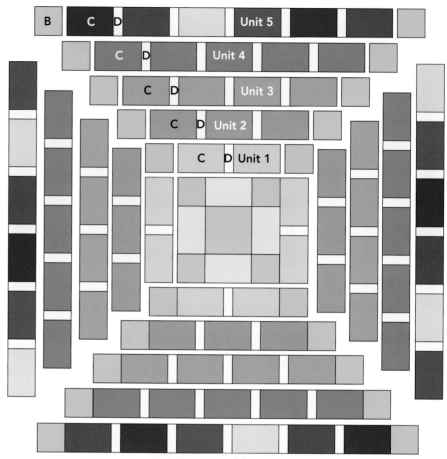

Quilt Top Assembly Diagram

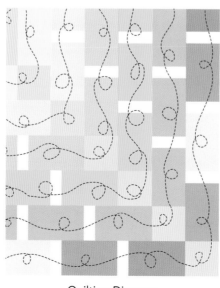

Quilting Diagram

DESIGNER

Anne Gallo and Susan Raban are well-known for their colorful, geometric quilts. They have developed a series of classes which they teach individually or as a team—always with an emphasis on precise machine piecing.

Contact them at:

Yankee Quilts • (603) 883-6641

anniegallo@comcast.net • susanraban@comcast.net ☀

Sedona Skies

The red rocks of Sedona, Arizona inspired designer Barbara Campbell to make this quilt in rich, southwestern colors. Because it has just a few blocks, you can finish it quickly.

Size: 56½" × 69½"
Blocks:
15 (10") Square-in-a-Square blocks
12 (8¼") Birds in the Air blocks

MATERIALS

1 yard gray print for blocks
   and borders
¾ yard rust print for blocks
   and sashing
¾ yard tan print for blocks
1⅜ yards maroon/gold print for
   blocks and binding
⅝ yard turquoise print for blocks
¼ yard dark brown print
   for blocks
½ yard red print for blocks
¼ yard medium brown print
   for blocks
¼ yard blue print for sashing
¼ yard green print for sashing
3½ yards backing fabric
Twin-size quilt batting

NOTE: Fabrics in the quilt shown are from the Paint Box Earthtones collection by Lonni Rossi for Andover Fabrics.

Cutting

Measurements include ¼" seam allowances. Border strips are exact length needed. You may want to make them longer to allow for piecing variations.

From gray print, cut:

- 7 (4"-wide) strips. From 1 strip, cut 8 (4") A squares. Piece remaining strips to make 2 (4" × 63") side borders and 2 (4" × 57") top and bottom borders.

From rust print, cut:

- 2 (4"-wide) strips. From strips, cut 18 (4") A squares.
- 6 (2½"-wide) strips. Piece strips to make 4 (2½" × 50") sashing rectangles.

From tan print, cut:

- 2 (4"-wide) strips. From strips, cut 20 (4") A squares.
- 2 (5⅞"-wide) strips. From strips, cut 10 (5⅞") squares. Cut squares in half diagonally to make 20 half-square B triangles.

From maroon/gold print, cut:

- 4 (5⅞"-wide) strips. From strips, cut 20 (5⅞") squares. Cut squares in half diagonally to make 40 half-square B triangles.
- 1 (4"-wide) strip. From strip, cut 10 (4") A squares.
- 7 (2¼"-wide) strips for binding.

From turquoise print, cut:

- 2 (9⅛"-wide) strips. From strips, cut 6 (9⅛") squares. Cut squares in half diagonally to make 12 half-square C triangles.

From dark brown print, cut:

- 2 (3⅝"-wide) strips. From strips, cut 18 (3⅝") squares. Cut squares in half diagonally to make 36 half-square D triangles.

From red print, cut:

- 4 (3⅝"-wide) strips. From strips, cut 36 (3⅝") squares. Cut squares in half diagonally to make 72 half-square D triangles.

From medium brown print, cut:

- 1 (4"-wide) strip. From strip, cut 4 (4") A squares.

From blue print, cut:

- 3 (2½"-wide) strips. Piece strips to make 2 (2½" × 50") sashing rectangles.

From green print, cut:

- 3 (2½"-wide) strips. Piece strips to make 2 (2½" × 50") sashing rectangles.

Square-In-A-Square Row Assembly

1. Join 2 rust print A squares and 2 tan print A squares as shown in *Four Patch Unit Diagrams*. Make 6 rust and tan Four Patch Units.

Four Patch Unit Diagrams

2. In the same manner make 4 gray and tan Four Patch Units, 2 medium brown and maroon/gold Four Patch Units, and 3 rust and maroon/gold Four Patch Units, using remaining A squares.

3. Lay out 4 maroon/gold print B triangles and 1 rust and tan Four Patch Unit as shown in *Square-in-a-Square Block Assembly Diagram*. Join to complete 1 Square-in-a Square block (*Square-in-a-Square Block Diagram*). Make 6 rust and tan Square-in-a-Square blocks.

4. In the same manner, make 4 Square-in-a-Square blocks using gray and tan Four Patch Units and maroon/gold B triangles, 3 Square-in-a-Square blocks using rust and maroon/gold Four

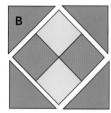

Square-in-a-Square Block Assembly Diagram

Square-in-a-Square Block Diagram

Patch Units and tan print B triangles, and 2 Square-in-a-Square blocks using medium brown and maroon/gold Four Patch Units and tan print B triangles.

5. Referring to *Quilt Top Assembly Diagram*, join 5 Square-in-a-Square blocks as shown to make 1 Square-in-a-Square row. Make 3 Square-in-a-Square rows.

Birds in the Air Row Assembly

1. Join 1 red print D triangle and 1 dark brown print D triangle as shown in *Triangle-Square Diagrams*. Make 36 red/dark brown triangle-squares.

Triangle-Square Diagrams

2. Referring to *Birds in the Air Block Assembly Diagram*, join 3 triangle-squares, 3 red print D triangles, and 1 turquoise print C triangle as shown to complete 1 Birds in the Air block (*Birds in the Air Block Diagram*). Make 12 Birds in the Air blocks.

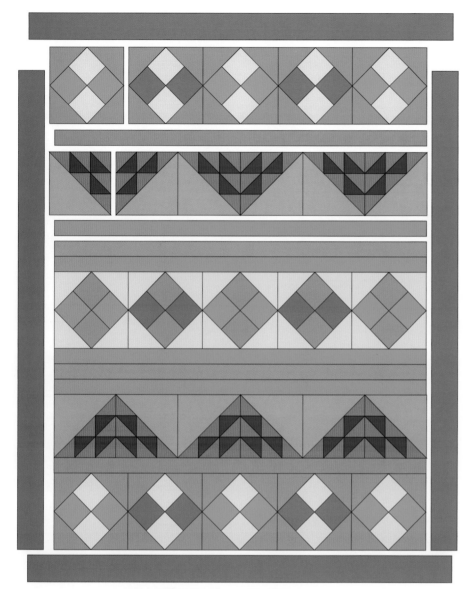

Quilt Top Assembly Diagram

Finishing

1. Divide backing into 2 (1¾-yard) lengths. Join panels lengthwise. Seam will run horizontally.

2. Layer backing, batting, and quilt top; baste. Quilt as desired. Quilt shown was quilted with an overall design *(Quilting Diagram)*.

3. Join 2¼"-wide maroon/gold print strips into 1 continuous piece for straight-grain French-fold binding. Add binding to quilt.

Quilting Diagram

Birds in the Air Block Assembly Diagram

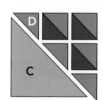

Birds in the Air Block Assembly Diagram

3. Join 6 Birds in the Air blocks to make 1 Birds in the Air row as shown in *Quilt Top Assembly Diagram*. Make 2 Birds in the Air rows.

Quilt Assembly

1. Lay out rows and sashing rectangles as shown in *Quilt Top Assembly Diagram*. Join rows to complete quilt center.

2. Add gray print side borders to quilt center. Add top and bottom borders to quilt.

TRIED & TRUE

Use small prints and primary colors to make a child's quilt. Fabrics shown are from the Noah's Ark collection by Sunshine Cottage for Northcott.

DESIGNER

Barbara Campbell is a quilt and pattern designer from Pine Brook, New Jersey. She enjoys exploring new techniques and loves the challenge of designing with new fabric lines that force her out of her comfort zone.

Contact her at: www.loveinstitches.com ✳

QUILT BY **Shon McMain**. MACHINE QUILTED BY **De Gillette**.

Tropical Twist

Use your batik stash to make simple blocks from easy-to-cut squares and rectangles. Twist and turn the blocks to create this bright, splashy quilt.

Size: 72¾" × 98¼"
Blocks: 59 (9") blocks

MATERIALS

25 fat quarters★ assorted bright
   batiks for blocks and binding
2⅜ yards dark orange batik for
   setting triangles and outer border
⅝ yard light orange batik for inner
   border
6 yards backing fabric
Queen-size quilt batting
★fat quarter = 18" × 20"

NOTE: Fabrics in the quilt shown are
Tonga batiks from Timeless Treasures.

Cutting

Measurements include ¼" seam allowances. Border strips are exact length needed. You may want to make them longer to allow for piecing variations.

From each fat quarter, cut:
- 1 (5"-wide) strip. From strip, cut
  2 (5" × 6½") A rectangles and
  2 (5" × 3½") B rectangles.
- 3 (3½"-wide) strips. From strips, cut 1
  (3½" × 9½") C rectangle,
  4 (3½" × 6½") D rectangles, and
  4 (3½" × 3½") E squares.
- 1 (2¼"-wide) strip for binding.

From dark orange batik, cut:
- 3 (14"-wide) strips. From strips, cut
  5 (14") squares. Cut squares in half
  diagonally in both directions to make
  20 side setting triangles.
- 1 (7¼"-wide) strip. From strip, cut
  2 (7¼") squares. Cut squares in half
  diagonally to make 4 corner setting
  triangles.
- 9 (3½"-wide) strips. Piece strips to
  make 2 (3½" × 92¾") side outer
  borders and 2 (3½" × 73¼") top and
  bottom outer borders.

From light orange batik, cut:

- 9 (2"-wide) strips. Piece strips to make 2 (2" × 89¾") side inner borders and 2 (2" × 67") top and bottom inner borders.

Block 1 Assembly

1. Lay out 2 A rectangles and 2 B rectangles as shown in *Block 1 Assembly Diagram*.

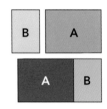

Block 1 Assembly Diagram

2. Join pieces to complete Block 1 (*Block 1 Diagram*). Make 20 Block 1.

Sew Smart™

For even more variety, change positions of squares and rectangles within some of the blocks.
—Marianne

Block 1 Assembly Diagram

Block 2 Assembly

1. Lay out 1 C rectangle, 1 D rectangle, and 4 E squares as shown in *Block 2 Assembly Diagram*.

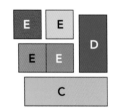

Block 2 Assembly Diagram

2. Join pieces to complete Block 2 (*Block 2 Diagram*). Make 19 Block 2.

Block 2 Diagram

Block 3 Assembly

1. Lay out 4 D rectangles and 1 E square as shown in *Block 3 Assembly Diagram*.

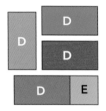

Block 3 Assembly Diagram

2. Join pieces to complete Block 3 (*Block 3 Diagram*). Make 20 Block 3.

Block 3 Diagram

Quilt Assembly

1. Referring to *Quilt Top Assembly Diagram*, lay out blocks, setting triangles, and corner triangles. Join into diagonal rows; joing rows to complete quilt center.

2. Add light orange batik side inner borders to quilt center. Add top and bottom inner borders to quilt.

3. Repeat for dark orange batik outer borders.

Finishing

1. Divide backing fabric into 2 (3-yard) lengths. Cut 1 piece in half lengthwise to make 2 narrow panels.

Join 1 narrow panel to each side of wider panel; press seam allowances toward narrow panels.

2. Layer backing, batting, and quilt top; baste. Quilt as desired. Quilt shown was quilted with an allover freehand design (*Quilting Diagram*).

3. Join 2¼"-wide assorted strips into 1 continuous piece for straight-grain French-fold binding. Add binding to quilt.

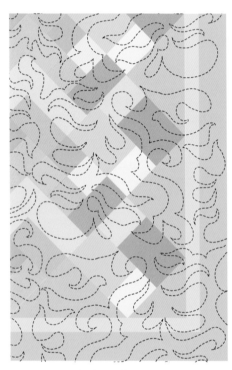

Quilting Diagram

Quilt Top Assembly Diagram

TRIED & TRUE

We made this cheery table topper using fabrics from the Verandah collection by Ro Gregg for Northcott.

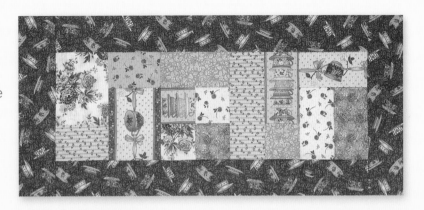

SIZE OPTIONS

	Crib (47¼" × 60")	Throw (60" × 72¾")	Full/Queen (98¼" × 98¼")
Block 1	4	9	26
Block 2	7	9	26
Block 3	7	14	33

MATERIALS

	Crib (47¼" × 60")	Throw (60" × 72¾")	Full/Queen (98¼" × 98¼")
Assorted Bright Batiks	11 fat quarters	18 fat quarters	40 fat quarters
Dark Orange Batik	1¾ yards	1⅞ yards	2¾ yards
Light Orange Batik	⅜ yard	½ yard	¾ yard
Backing Fabric	3 yards	3¾ yards	8¾ yards
Batting	Twin-size	Twin-size	King-size

 WEB EXTRA

Go to www.FonsandPorter.com/tropicalsizes to download *Quilt Top Assembly Diagrams* for these size options.

DESIGNER

Whether she's choosing fabrics, creating original designs, piecing, or quilting, designer Shon McMain loves every aspect of making quilts. Most of her quilts are made from batiks, her favorite fabrics. Shon lives in Des Moines, Iowa.

Contact her at: dgillette@aol.com ✳

QUILT BY **Jean-Anne Sharrai**.

Paisley on Point

Choose a large-scale floral fabric for the border and coordinating fabrics for the easy Four Patch Units and squares. You'll finish this fantastic quilt in no time at all.

Size: 67" × 84"

MATERIALS

2 yards large-scale cranberry print

1 yard moss print #1

½ yard moss print #2

½ yard cranberry print #1

½ yard cranberry print #2

1¼ yards light gold print

1 yard paisley print

Fons & Porter Easy Diagonal Sets
   Ruler (optional)

5 yards backing fabric

Twin-size quilt batting

NOTE: Fabrics in the quilt shown are from the Aspen collection by Marianne Elizabeth for Benartex.

Cutting

Measurements include ¼" seam allowances. Border strips are exact length needed. You may want to make them longer to allow for piecing variations.

NOTE: Cutting Instructions are for use with the Fons & Porter Easy Diagonal Sets Ruler. If you are NOT using this ruler, read through all instructions before beginning to cut.

From large-scale cranberry print, cut:

• 8 (8½"-wide) strips. Piece strips to make 2 (8½" × 68½") side borders and 2 (8½" × 67½") top and bottom borders.

From moss print #1, cut:

• 4 (3½"-wide) strips for strip sets.

• 9 (2¼"-wide) strips for binding.

From moss print #2, cut:

• 4 (3½"-wide) strips for strip sets.

From cranberry print #1, cut:

• 4 (3½"-wide) strips for strip sets.

From cranberry print #2, cut:

• 4 (3½"-wide) strips for strip sets.

From light gold print, cut:
- 2 (6½"-wide) strips. From strips, cut 12 (6½") squares.
- 4 (4¾"-wide) strips. From strips, cut 28 side setting triangles. (See *Sew Easy: Cutting Setting Triangles* on page 111.)

If NOT using the Fons & Porter Easy Diagonal Sets Ruler to cut the setting triangles, cut:
- 2 (9¾"-wide) strips. From strips, cut 7 (9¾") squares. Cut squares in half diagonally in both directions to make 28 quarter-square setting triangles.

From paisley print, cut:
- 5 (6½"-wide) strips. From strips, cut 28 (6½") squares.

Four Patch Unit Assembly

1. Join 1 moss print #1 strip and 1 cranberry print #1 strip as shown in *Strip Set Diagram*. Make 4 Strip Sets. From strip sets, cut 42 (3½"-wide) segments.

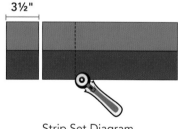

3½"

Strip Set Diagram

2. Join 2 segments as shown in *Four Patch Unit Diagrams*. Make 21 Four Patch Units.

Four Patch Unit Diagrams

3. In the same manner, make 21 Four Patch Units using moss print #2 and cranberry print #2.

Quilt Assembly

1. Lay out Four Patch Units, paisley print squares, light gold print squares, and setting triangles, as shown in *Quilt Top Assembly Diagram*.

2. Join into diagonal rows; join rows to complete quilt center.

3. Add cranberry print side borders to quilt center. Add top and bottom borders to quilt.

Finishing

1. Divide backing into 2 (2½-yard) lengths. Cut 1 piece in half lengthwise to make 2 narrow panels. Join 1 narrow panel to each side of wider panel; press seam allowances toward narrow panels.

2. Layer backing, batting, and quilt top; baste. Quilt as desired. Quilt shown was quilted with an allover vine and leaf design *(Quilting Diagram)*.

3. Join 2¼"-wide moss print #1 strips into 1 continuous piece for straight-grain French-fold binding. Add binding to quilt.

Quilting Diagram

Quilt Top Assembly Diagram

DESIGNER

Jean-Anne Sharrai has been designing quilts for more than 20 years, and was a family consumer sciences teacher at the high school level for fifteen years. She now combines two of her passions, teaching and quilting. ✳

Cutting Setting Triangles

With the Fons & Porter Easy Diagonal Sets Ruler, cutting the side and corner setting triangles for diagonally set quilts is a snap—all the math is done for you! Cut side and corner setting triangles from the same size strip.

Cutting Corner Setting Triangles

1. On the Diagonal Sets Ruler, find the yellow line that corresponds to your finished block size.
2. Cut a strip that width.
3. Cut corner setting triangles from strip by first aligning the yellow cutting guideline along bottom edge of cut strip and then along top edge (Photo B).

Sew Smart™

Use the same width strip to cut both the side and corner setting triangles. If you are short on fabric, first cut a corner setting triangle (yellow lines) from the strip; then, cut the remainder of the strip into side setting triangles and finish by cutting a corner setting triangle.
—Liz

Cutting Side Setting Triangles

1. On the Diagonal Sets Ruler, find the black line that corresponds to your finished block size. The Four-Patch blocks in Paisley on Point are 6" finished.
2. Cut a fabric strip the width indicated along the edge of the ruler. For the Side Setting Triangles in Paisley or Point, cut strips 4¾" wide.

Sew Smart™

If your blocks finish in a fraction of an inch or you want to "float" your blocks in a diagonal set, use the next largest block size.
—Marianne

3. Open out strip so you will cut through a single layer. From strip, cut side setting triangles by first placing the black cutting guideline along bottom edge of strip, then top edge (Photo A).

Garden Gate

Soft sage green and rose flowered fabrics create this quilted garden crisscrossed by patchwork stepping stones.

Size: 90½" × 107½"
Blocks: 20 (12") blocks

MATERIALS

3 yards green stripe for border
1 yard green print for border
3 yards beige floral print for setting squares and triangles
⅝ yard light beige print for blocks
1 yard medium beige print for blocks
1⅜ yards dark beige print for blocks
¼ yard pink print for blocks
⅜ yard light rose print for blocks
¾ yard medium rose print for blocks and border
1½ yards dark rose print for blocks, border, and binding
8¼ yards backing fabric
King-size quilt batting

NOTE: Fabrics in the quilt shown are from the Garden collections by Ro Gregg for Northcott.

Cutting

Measurements include ¼" seam allowances.

From green stripe, cut:
- 11 (8¼"-wide) strips. Piece strips to make 2 (8¼" × 112") side borders and 2 (8¼" × 95") top and bottom borders.

From green print, cut:
- 11 (2½"-wide) strips. Piece strips to make 2 (2½" × 112") side borders and 2 (2½" × 95") top and bottom borders.

From beige floral print, cut:
- 2 (18¼"-wide) strips. From strips cut 4 (18¼") squares. Cut squares in half diagonally in both directions to make 16 side setting triangles (2 are extra).
- 4 (12½"-wide) strips. From strips cut 12 (12½") setting squares.
- 1 (9⅜"-wide) strip. From strip, cut 2 (9⅜") squares. Cut squares in half diagonally to make 4 corner setting triangles.

From light beige print, cut:
- 4 (3½"-wide) strips. From 2 strips, cut 40 (3½" × 2") B rectangles. Remaining strips are for strip sets.

From medium beige print, cut:
- 4 (6½"-wide) strips. From 2 strips, cut 40 (6½" × 2") C rectangles. Remaining strips are for strip sets.

From dark beige print, cut:
- 4 (9½"-wide) strips. From 2 strips, cut 40 (9½" × 2") D rectangles. Remaining strips are for strip sets.

From pink print, cut:
- 2 (3½"-wide) strips. From strips, cut 20 (3½") A squares.

From light rose print, cut:
- 4 (2"-wide) strips for strip sets.

From medium rose print, cut:
- 4 (2"-wide) strips for strip sets.
- 11 (1¼"-wide) strips. Piece strips to make 2 (1¼" × 112") side borders and 2 (1¼" × 95") top and bottom borders.

From dark rose print, cut:
- 11 (2¼"-wide) strips for binding.
- 4 (2"-wide) strips for strip sets.
- 11 (1¼"-wide) strips. Piece strips to make 2 (1¼" × 112") side borders and 2 (1¼" × 95") top and bottom borders.

Block Assembly

1. Join 2 light rose print strips and 1 light beige print strip to make 1 Strip Set #1 *(Strip Set Diagrams)*. Make 2 Strip Set #1. From strip sets, cut 40 (2"-wide) #1 segments.

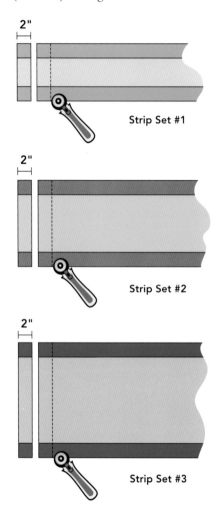

Strip Set Diagrams

2. In the same manner, join 2 medium rose print strips and 1 medium beige print strip to make 1 Strip Set #2. Make 2 Strip Set #2. From strip sets, cut 40 (2"-wide) #2 segments.

3. In the same manner, join 2 dark rose print strips and 1 dark beige print strip to make 1 Strip Set #3. Make 2 Strip Set #3. From strip sets, cut 40 (2"-wide) #3 segments.

4. Lay out 1 pink print A square, 2 light beige print B rectangles, 2 medium beige print C rectangles, 2 dark beige print D rectangles, 2 Segment #1, 2 Segment #2, and 2 Segment #3 as shown in *Block Assembly Diagrams.* Join to complete 1 block *(Block Diagram)*. Make 20 blocks.

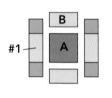

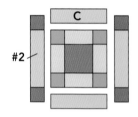

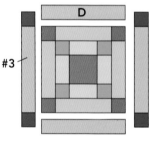

Block Assembly Diagrams

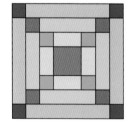

Block Diagram

Quilt Assembly

1. Lay out blocks, setting squares, and setting triangles as shown in *Quilt Top Assembly Diagram.* Join into diagonal rows; join rows to complete quilt center.

2. Join 1 medium rose print side border, 1 green print side border, 1 dark rose print side border, and 1 green stripe side border, matching centers, to make 1 side border strip set. Make 2 side border strip sets.

3. In the same manner, make top and bottom border strip sets.

4. Add border strip sets to quilt, mitering corners.

🖱 **WEB** EXTRA

For instructions on mitering borders visit our Web site at www.FonsandPorter.com/ mborders.

Finishing

1. Divide backing into 3 (2¾-yard) lengths. Join panels lengthwise. Seam will run horizontally.

2. Layer backing, batting, and quilt top; baste. Quilt as desired. Quilt shown was quilted with a leaf design in pieced blocks, rose design in setting blocks and triangles, quilted in the ditch between borders, and outline quilted around design in green stripe border *(Quilting Diagram on page 117)*.

3. Join 2¼"-wide dark rose print strips into 1 continuous piece for straight-grain French-fold binding. Add binding to quilt.

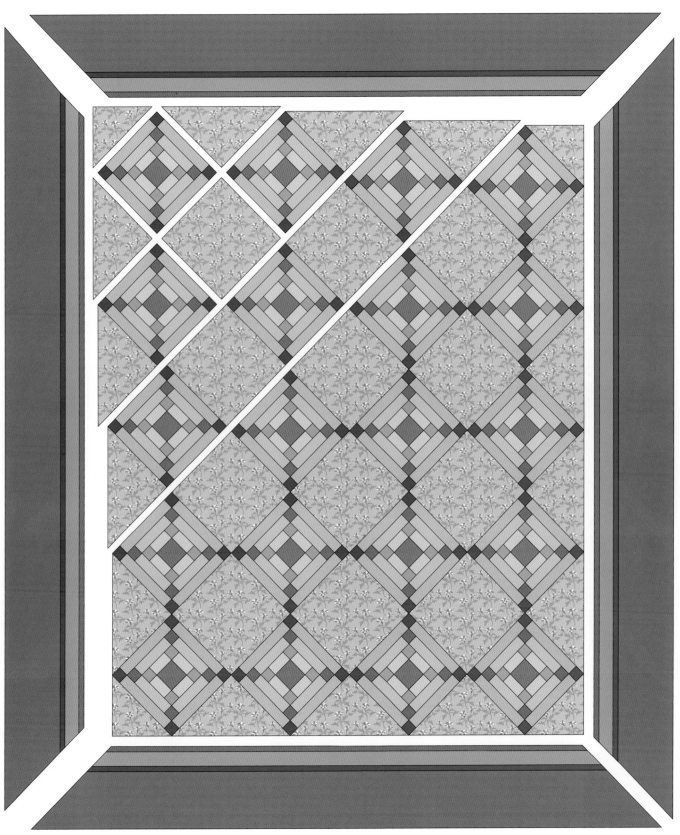

Quilt Top Assembly Diagram

SIZE OPTION

	Twin (73½" × 90½")
Blocks	12

MATERIALS

Green Stripe	2½ yards
Green Print	¾ yard
Beige Floral Print	2¼ yards
Light Beige Print	½ yard
Medium Beige Print	⅞ yard
Dark Beige Print	1¼ yards
Pink Print	¼ yard
Light Rose Print	⅜ yard
Medium Rose Print	⅝ yard
Dark Rose Print	1¼ yards
Backing Fabric	5½ yard
Batting	Full-size

DESIGNER

Patti Carey enjoys playing with new fabrics designing quilts that inspire other quilters.

Contact her at:

patti.carey@northcott.net ✳

WEB EXTRA

Go to www.FonsandPorter.com/gardengatesizes to download *Quilt Top Assembly Diagrams* for these size options.

Quilting Diagram

TRIED & TRUE

The soft, subtle tones in the Sea Etchings fabrics by Ro Gregg for Northcott are just right for an underwater garden version of this quilt.

Heavenly Hollyhocks

Designer Patti Carey used a printed panel to create this quick and easy wallhanging that's perfect for summer decorating.

Size: 45" × 49"

MATERIALS

¾ yard Heavenly Hollyhocks panel print

½ yard light tan print for border #1

¼ yard red print for border #2

¼ yard pink print for border #3

⅝ yard tan floral for border #4

¼ yard light green print for border #5

¾ yard dark green print for border #6 and binding

3 yards backing fabric

Twin-size quilt batting

NOTE: Fabrics in the quilt shown are from the Heavenly Hollyhocks collection by Lain Stowe for Northcott.

Cutting

Measurements include ¼" seam allowances. Border strips are exact length needed. You may want to make them longer to allow for piecing variations.

From Heavenly Hollyhocks panel print, cut:

- 3 (8" × 32½") A rectangles.
  NOTE: Refer to photo on page 118. Cut approximately ½" below bottom of printed stems.

From light tan print, cut:

- 2 (3¼"-wide) strips. From strips, cut 2 (3¼" × 32½") B rectangles.
- 4 (1½"-wide) strips. From strips, cut 2 (1½" × 32½") side border #1 and 2 (1½" × 30½") top and bottom border #1.

From red print, cut:

- 4 (1¼"-wide) strips. From strips, cut 2 (1¼" × 34½") side border #2 and 2 (1¼" × 32") top and bottom border #2.

From pink print, cut:

- 4 (1"-wide) strips. From strips, cut 2 (1" × 36") side border #3 and 2 (1" × 33") top and bottom border #3.

From tan floral print, cut:

- 4 (4½"-wide) strips. From strips, cut 2 (4½" × 41") top and bottom border #4 and 2 (4½" × 37") side border #4.

From light green print, cut:

- 5 (1¼"-wide) strips. Piece strips to make 2 (1¼" × 45") side border #5 and 2 (1¼" × 42½") top and bottom border #5.

From dark green print, cut:

- 6 (2¼"-wide) strips for binding.
- 5 (2"-wide) strips. Piece strips to make 2 (2" × 46½") side border #6 and 2 (2" × 45½") top and bottom border #6.

#6

#5

#4

#3

#2

#1

A

B

Quilt Top Assembly Diagram

Quilt Assembly

1. Lay out panel print A rectangles and 2 light tan print B rectangles as shown in *Quilt Top Assembly Diagram*. Join rectangles to complete quilt center.

2. Add light tan print side border #1 to quilt center. Add top and bottom border #1 to quilt.

3. Repeat for remaining borders.

Finishing

1. Divide backing into 2 (1½-yard) lengths. Cut 1 piece in half lengthwise to make 2 narrow panels. Join 1 narrow panel to wider panel. Remaining panel is extra and can be used to make a hanging sleeve.

2. Layer backing, batting, and quilt top; baste. Quilt as desired. Quilt shown was outline quilted around the hollyhock design in quilt center, quilted in the ditch between borders, and has a feather design in tan border #4 and a leaf design in border #6 *(Quilting Diagram)*.

3. Join 2¼"-wide dark green print strips into 1 continuous piece for straight-grain French-fold binding. Add binding to quilt. ✳

Quilting Diagram

DESIGNER

Patti Carey enjoys playing with new fabrics designing quilts that inspire other quilters.

Contact her at:
patti.carey@northcott.net ✳

Pinwheel Posies

This delightful quilt features rows of pinwheel flowers accented with yo-yos and buttons. You can stitch the large blocks in just a few hours.

Size: 75" × 87"
Blocks: 20 (12") Pinwheel blocks

MATERIALS

3¾ yards aqua print for blocks, outer border, and binding
1 yard yellow print for inner border and yo-yos
1 yard pink print for blocks
1½ yards white print for blocks
½ yard each of 4 assorted prints in blue, green, and aqua for blocks
5½ yards backing fabric
Full-size quilt batting
20 (1"-diameter) white buttons
Clover large-size Yo-Yo Maker (optional)

NOTE: Fabrics in the quilt shown are from the Lava Group collection by Michael Miller Fabrics.

Cutting

Measurements include ¼" seam allowances. Border strips are exact length needed. You may want to make them longer to allow for piecing variations. Pattern for yo-yo circle is on page 127.

From aqua print, cut:
• 2 (7¼"-wide) strips. From strips, cut 10 (7¼") squares. Cut squares in half diagonally in both directions to make 40 quarter-square A triangles.
• 6 (6⅞"-wide) strips. From strips, cut 28 (6⅞") squares. Cut squares in half diagonally to make 56 half-square B triangles.
• 8 (6½"-wide) strips. Piece strips to make 2 (6½" × 75½") top and bottom outer borders and 2 (6½" × 75½") side outer borders.
• 9 (2¼"-wide) strips for binding.

From yellow print, cut:
• 8 (2"-wide) strips. Piece strips to make 2 (2" × 72½") side inner borders and 2 (2" × 63½") top and bottom inner borders.
• 20 Yo-Yo Circles.

From pink print, cut:

• 4 (7¼"-wide) strips. From strips, cut 20 (7¼") squares. Cut squares in half diagonally in both directions to make 80 quarter-square A triangles.

From white print, cut:

• 6 (7¼"-wide) strips. From strips, cut 30 (7¼") squares. Cut squares in half diagonally in both directions to make 120 quarter-square A triangles.

From each assorted print, cut:

• 2 (6⅞"-wide) strips. From strips, cut 8 (6⅞") squares. Cut squares in half diagonally to make 16 half-square B triangles.

Block Assembly

1. Join 1 white print A triangle, 1 pink print A triangle, and 1 green print B triangle as shown in *Pinwheel Unit Diagrams.* Make 4 Pinwheel Units.

Pinwheel Unit Diagrams

2. In the same manner, make 19 sets of 4 matching Pinwheel Units using assorted print B triangles, white print A triangles, and pink print A triangles. Make 40 Pinwheel Units using aqua print A and B triangles and white print A triangles.

3. Lay out 4 matching Pinwheel Units as shown in *Block Assembly Diagram.* Join into rows; join rows to complete 1 Pinwheel block *(Block Diagram).* Make 20 blocks.

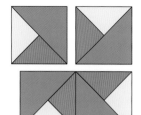

Block Assembly Diagram

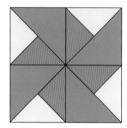

Block Diagram

Quilt Assembly

1. Lay out blocks as shown in *Quilt Top Assembly Diagram.* Join into rows; join rows to complete quilt center.

2. Join 10 aqua Pinwheel Units as shown to make 1 pieced side border. Make 2 pieced side borders. Add borders to quilt center.

3. Join 10 aqua Pinwheel Units as shown to make pieced top border. Repeat for bottom border. Add borders to quilt.

4. Add yellow print side inner borders to quilt. Add top and bottom inner borders to quilt.

5. Repeat for aqua print outer borders.

Finishing

1. Divide backing into 2 (2¾-yard) lengths. Cut 1 piece in half lengthwise to make 2 narrow panels. Join 1 narrow panel to each side of wider panel; press seam allowances toward narrow panels.

2. Layer backing, batting, and quilt top; baste. Quilt as desired. Quilt shown was quilted with an allover bouquet design *(Quilting Diagram).*

Quilting Diagram

3. Referring to *Sew Easy: Making Yo-Yos* on page 127, make 20 yellow print yo-yos.

> **Sew Smart™**
> A yo-yo maker makes quick work of making yo-yos. —Liz

4. Place yo-yos atop blocks as shown in photo on page 123. Sew a button in center of each yo-yo, stitching through all layers.

5. Join 2¼"-wide aqua print strips into 1 continuous piece for straight-grain French-fold binding. Add binding to quilt.

Quilt Top Assembly Diagram

TRIED & TRUE

The sophisticated batiks from Tonga Batiks by Timeless Treasures are enhanced by a teal Yo-yo and lavender button.

SIZE OPTIONS

	Crib (51" × 51")	Twin (63" × 99")	Queen (99" × 99")
Blocks	4	18	36
Setting	2 × 2	3 × 6	6 × 6
MATERIALS			
Aqua print	2 yards	3½ yards	4¾ yards
Yellow print	½ yard	1 yard	1¾ yards
Pink print	¼ yard	1 yard	1¾ yards
White print	½ yard	1⅜ yards	2¼ yards
4 Assorted prints	1 fat eighth each★	½ yard each	1 yard each
Backing Fabric	3 yards	6 yards	9 yards
Batting	Twin–size	Queen–size	King–size

★fat eighth = 9" × 20"

WEB EXTRA

Go to www.FonsandPorter.com/pinposiessizes to download *Quilt Top Assembly Diagrams* for these size options.

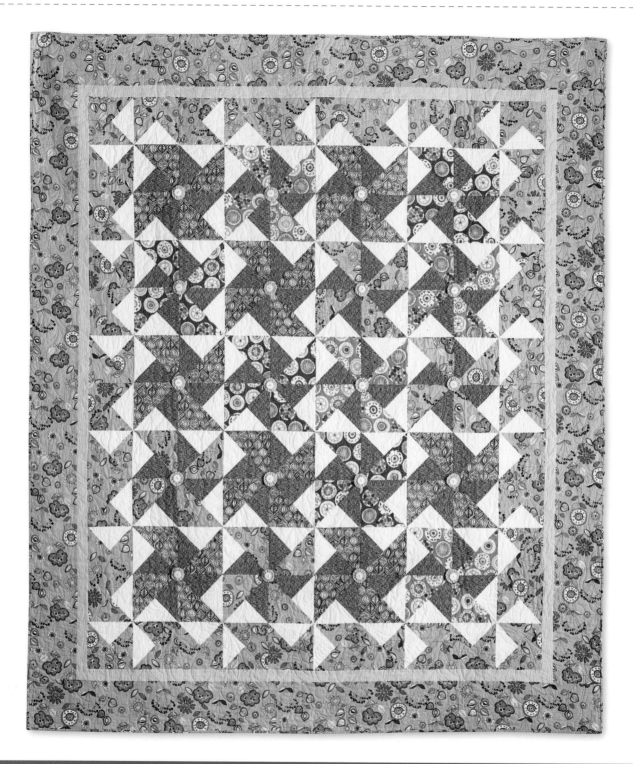

DESIGNER

Susan Emory and Christine Van Buskirk of Swirly Girls Design pattern company combine Susan's graphic arts background with Christine's engineering skills to create visually appealing quilts with efficient, accurate instructions. Susan is the owner of Quilter's Corner in Midlothian, Virginia, and Christine is the manager. They both teach classes for quilters of all skill levels.

Contact them at: Swirly Girls Design • 1257 Sycamore Square, Midlothian, VA 23113 • (804) 647-8770
www.swirlygirlsdesign.com ✳

Making Yo-Yos

Follow these simple steps to make yo-yos for *Pinwheel Posies* on page 122.

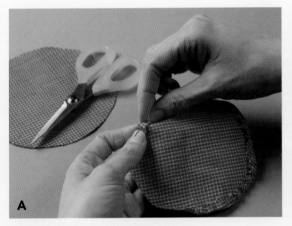

A

B

1. Cut circle using Yo-Yo Circle pattern.
2. Turn under raw edge of circle ¼" to wrong side and take small running stitches around edge through both layers *(Photo A)*. Use quilting thread or other strong thread that will not break when gathering.
3. Pull thread to gather circle with right side of fabric facing out. Make a knot to hold circle closed. Gathered side is front of yo-yo *(Photo B)*.

Sew Smart™
Do not make running stitches too small. Longer stitches make the circle easier to gather, and the "hole" smaller. —Marianne

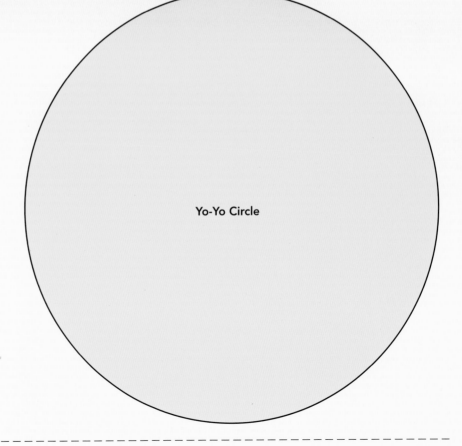

Yo-Yo Circle

Are you wishing for spring to arrive? Make this cute wallhanging while you wait.

Size: 22" × 42"
Blocks: 8 (4") Pinwheel blocks

MATERIALS

½ yard yellow print for background

½ yard pink print for letters, pinwheels, sashing, and inner border

3 fat eighths★★ pink prints for pinwheels

1 fat quarter★ light green print for pinwheels

1 fat quarter★ light green stripe for squares

¾ yard brown print for outer border and binding

2 (8") squares gold prints for circles

2 (8") squares dark green prints for stems and leaves

3 (⅞"-diameter) yellow buttons

Paper-backed fusible web

1⅜ yards backing fabric.

Craft-size quilt batting

★fat quarter = 18" × 20"

★★fat eighth = 9" × 20"

NOTE: Fabrics in the quilt shown are from the Millie's Garden collection by Tammy Johnson & Avis Shirer of Joined at the Hip for Clothworks™.

Cutting

Measurements include ¼" seam allowances. Border strips are exact length needed. You may want to make them longer to allow for piecing variations. Patterns for appliqué are on page 132. Follow manufacturer's instructions for using fusible web.

From yellow print, cut:

• 1 (7½"-wide) strip. From strip, cut
  1 (7½" × 16½") L rectangle,
  1 (4½" × 11½") K rectangle,
  1 (2½" × 4½") J rectangle, and
  1 (2½") I square.

• 2 (1½"-wide) strips. From strips, cut
  1 (1½" × 16½") H rectangle,
  1 (1½" × 8½") G rectangle,
  2 (1½" × 5½") F rectangles,
  2 (1½" × 3½") D rectangles,
  1 (1½" × 2½") C rectangle, and
  14 (1½") B squares.

From pink print, cut:

• 7 (1½"-wide) strips. From strips, cut
  2 (1½" × 36½") side inner borders,

2 (1½" × 18½") top and bottom inner borders, 3 (1½" × 16½") sashing rectangles, 2 (1½" × 8½") G rectangles, 2 (1½" × 5½") F rectangles, 1 (1½" × 4½") E rectangle, 10 (1½" × 3½") D rectangles, 8 (1½" × 2½") C rectangles, and 2 (1½") B squares.

From each pink print fat eighth, cut:

• 2 (1½"-wide) strips. From strips, cut 8 (1½" × 2½") C rectangles.

From remaining pink prints, cut:

• 3 Flowers.

From light green print, cut:

• 11 (1½"-wide) strips. From strips, cut 32 (1½" × 2½") C rectangles and 64 (1½") B squares.

From light green stripe, cut:

• 2 (4½"-wide) strips. From strips, cut 8 (4½") A squares.

From brown print, cut:

• 4 (2½"-wide) strips. From strips, cut 2 (2½" × 38½") side outer borders and 2 (2½" × 22½") top and bottom outer borders.

• 4 (2¼"-wide) strips for binding.

From gold prints, cut:

• 3 Circles.

From dark green prints, cut:

- 3 Stems.
- 6 Leaves.

Block Assembly

1. Referring to *Flying Geese Unit Diagrams*, place 1 light green print B square atop 1 pink print C rectangle, right sides facing. Stitch diagonally from corner to corner as shown. Trim ¼" beyond stitching. Press open to reveal triangle. Repeat for opposite end of rectangle to complete 1 Flying Geese Unit. Make 8 sets of 4 matching Flying Geese Units.

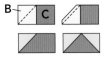

Flying Geese Unit Diagrams

2. Lay out 4 matching Flying Geese Units and 4 green print C rectangles as shown in *Block Assembly Diagram*. Join into sections, join sections to complete 1 block *(Block Diagram)*. Make 8 blocks.

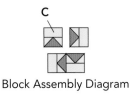

Block Assembly Diagram

Block Diagram

Pinwheel Section Assembly

1. Lay out 4 blocks and 4 light green stripe A squares as shown in *Quilt Top Assembly Diagram*.

2. Join into rows; join rows to complete 1 Pinwheel Section. Make 2 Pinwheel Sections.

Bloom Section Assembly

1. Referring to *Diagonal Seams Diagrams*, place 1 yellow print B square atop 1 pink print E rectangle, right sides facing. Stitch diagonally from corner to corner as shown. Trim ¼" beyond stitching. Press open to reveal triangle. Repeat for other end of rectangle to complete 1 Diagonal Seams Unit.

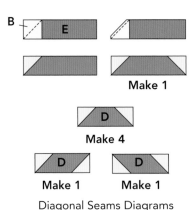

Make 1

Make 4

Make 1   Make 1

Diagonal Seams Diagrams

2. In a similar manner, make 6 Diagonal Seams Units using pink print D rectangles as shown,

3. Lay out 1 yellow print G rectangle, 2 pink print G rectangles, 2 pink print B squares, 1 yellow print C rectangle, 1 yellow print J rectangle, 1 yellow print F rectangle, and 1 Diagonal Seams Unit E as shown in *Bloom Section Diagrams*. Join to complete BL Unit.

4. In a similar manner, join 4 pink print D rectangles, 2 yellow print D rectangles, 2 pink print F rectangles, 1 yellow print F rectangle, 1 yellow print I square, and remaining Diagonal Seams Units as shown to complete OOM Unit.

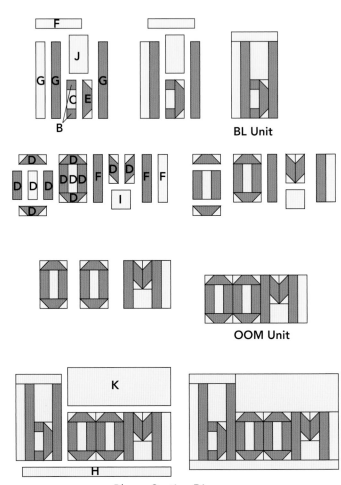

BL Unit

OOM Unit

Bloom Section Diagrams

5. Lay out BL and OOM Units, yellow print K rectangle, and yellow print H rectangle as shown. Join to complete Bloom Section.

Quilt Assembly

1. Lay out Pinwheel and Bloom Sections, yellow print L rectangle, and pink print sashing rectangles as shown in *Quilt Top Assembly Diagram*. Join to complete quilt center.

2. Arrange Flowers, Leaves, and Stems atop yellow print L rectangle as shown in photo on page 129. Fuse in place. Machine appliqué using blanket stitch and matching thread.

3. Add pink print side inner borders to quilt center. Add pink print top and bottom inner borders to quilt.

4. Repeat for brown print outer borders.

Finishing

1. Layer backing, batting, and quilt top; baste. Quilt as desired. Quilt shown was quilted in the ditch and with overall meandering *(Quilting Diagram)*.

2. Join 2¼"-wide brown print strips into 1 continuous piece for straight-grain French-fold binding. Add binding to quilt.

3. Sew a button in center of each flower.

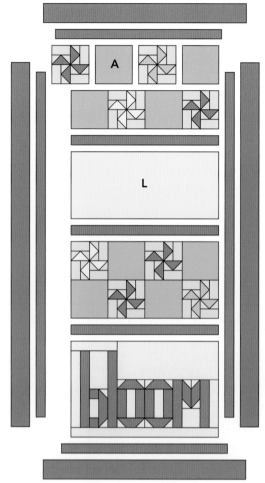

Quilt Top Assembly Diagram

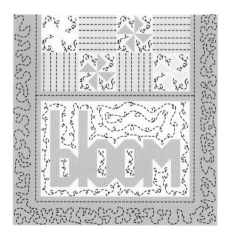

Quilting Diagram

TRIED & TRUE

Combine graphic black-and-white prints with bright colors for a bold look. Fabrics shown are from the Luna collection by Gail Fountain and Maywood Studio.

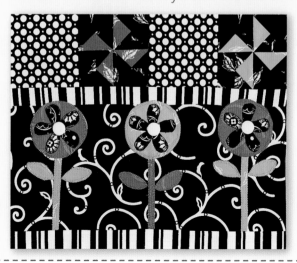

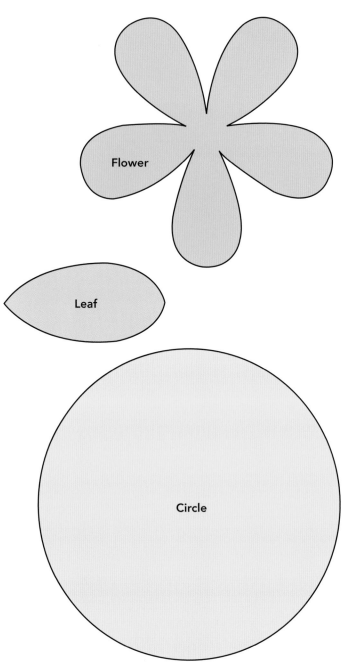

Flower

Leaf

Circle

Patterns are shown full size for use with fusible web. Add $^3/_{16}$" seam allowance for hand appliqué.

Stem

DESIGNER

Tammy Johnson is half of the design duo Joined at the Hip. Tammy and Avis Shirer have been designing quilts since 1997. They have self-published hundreds of patterns and thirteen books. They love to combine piecing and appliqué in their whimsical designs. Their love of nature and the changing seasons in Iowa are reflected in their patterns and fabric designs.

Contact her at:

www.joinedatthehip.com ✳

Autumn Posy Patch

Making this cute strippy quilt is easy as pie! Strip piecing and fusible appliqué make this a fun weekend project.

Size: 47½" × 61½"

MATERIALS

⅞ yard cream print

⅝ yard light tan print

1¼ yards pink print #1

⅜ yard pink print #2

1 fat eighth★ pink print #3

¼ yard brown dot

1 fat eighth★ brown print #1

⅜ yard brown print #2

¾ yard blue dot

1 fat eighth★ blue print

2 fat eighths★ light green prints for leaves

¼ yard orange print #1

⅜ yard orange print #2

¼ yard each of orange stripe and blue stripe prints

Paper-backed fusible web

3 yards backing fabric

10 (⅝"-diameter) star buttons

Full-size quilt batting

★fat eighth = 9" × 20"

NOTE: Fabrics in the quilt shown are from the Everything Autumn collection by Karla Eisenach of Sweetwater for Clothworks.

Cutting

Measurements include ¼" seam allowances. Border strips are exact length needed. You may want to make them longer to allow for piecing variations. Patterns for appliqué shapes and yo-yo circle are on pages 137 and 141. Follow manufacturer's instructions for using fusible web.

From cream print, cut:

• 8 (3"-wide) strips. Piece strips to make 6 (3" × 48½") strips.

From light tan print, cut:

• 5 (2½"-wide) strips. From 2 strips, cut 2 (2½" × 38½") top and bottom inner borders. Piece remaining strips to make 2 (2½" × 48½") side inner borders.

• 10 Yo-Yo Circles.

From pink print #1, cut:

• 6 (5¼"-wide) strips. Piece strips to make 2 (5¼" × 52½") side inner borders and 2 (5¼" × 48") top and bottom inner borders.

• 2 (2½"-wide) strips for strip sets.

From pink print #2, cut:

• 2 (2½"-wide) strips for strip sets.

• 2 Flowers.

From pink print #3, cut:

• 1 Flower.

From brown dot, cut:

• 4 (1½"-wide) strips. Piece strips to make 3 (1½" × 48½") stem strips.

From brown print #1, cut:

• 1 Flower.

From brown print #2, cut:

• 2 (2½"-wide) strips for strip sets.

• 1 Flower.

From blue dot, cut:

• 2 (2½"-wide) strips for strip sets.

• 6 (2¼"-wide) strips for binding.

• 1 Flower.

From blue print fat eighth, cut:

• 1 Flower.

From each light green print fat eighth, cut:

• 11 Leaves.

From orange print #1, cut:

• 2 (2½"-wide) strips for strip sets.

From orange print #2, cut:
- 2 (2½"-wide) strips for strip sets.
- 3 Flowers.

From each stripe print, cut:
- 2 (2½"-wide) strips for strip sets.

Quilt Center Assembly

1. Referring to *Strip Set A Diagram*, join 4 (2½"-wide) strips in this order from top to bottom: orange print #1, blue dot, blue stripe, and orange print #2. Make 2 Strip Set A. From strip sets, cut 24 (2½"-wide) A segments.

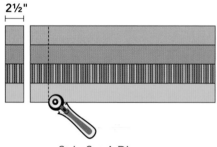

2½"

Strip Set A Diagram

2. Referring to *Strip Set B Diagram*, join 4 (2½"-wide) strips in this order from top to bottom: pink print #2, orange stripe, brown print #2, and pink print #1. Make 2 Strip Set B. From strip sets, cut 24 (2½"-wide) B segments.

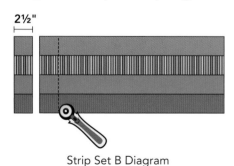

2½"

Strip Set B Diagram

3. Join 1 segment A and 1 segment B to make 1 section. Make 12 sections with segment A on the left and 12 sections with segment A on the right as shown in *Strippy Section Diagrams*.

Strippy Section Diagrams

4. Referring to *Quilt Top Assembly Diagram*, join 6 strippy sections (3 from each group), to make 1 strippy row. Make 4 strippy rows.

5. Add 1 (3" × 48½") cream print strip to each long side of 1 (1½" × 48½") brown dot stem strip to make 1 stem row. Make 3 stem rows.

6. Referring to *Quilt Top Assembly Diagram*, appliqué flowers and leaves on each stem row.

7. Referring to *Sew Easy: Making Yo-Yos* on page 141, make 10 light tan print yo-yos.

Quilt Assembly

1. Lay out strippy rows and stem rows as shown in *Quilt Top Assembly Diagram*. Join rows to complete quilt center.

2. Add beige side inner borders to quilt center. Add top and bottom inner borders to quilt. Repeat for pink print #1 outer borders.

Finishing

1. Divide backing fabric into 2 (1½-yard) lengths. Join pieces lengthwise. Seam will run horizontally.

Quilt Top Assembly Diagram

2. Layer backing, batting, and quilt top; baste. Quilt as desired. Quilt shown was quilted with loops in beige background and with a flower and leaf design in outer border *(Quilting Diagram)*.

Quilting Diagram

3. Place yo-yos atop flowers as shown in photo on page 139. Sew a button on each yo-yo, stitching through quilt top and batting only.

4. Join 2¼"-wide blue dot strips into 1 continuous piece for straight-grain French-fold binding. Add binding to quilt.

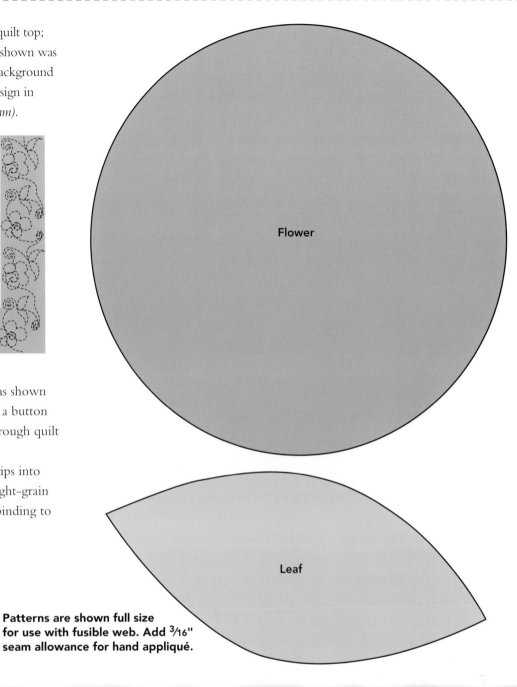

Flower

Leaf

Patterns are shown full size for use with fusible web. Add ³⁄16" seam allowance for hand appliqué.

SIZE OPTIONS

	Throw (57½" × 77½")	Twin (67½" × 93½")	Full (77½" × 93½")
Strippy Rows	5	6	7
Stem Rows	4	5	6

MATERIALS

Cream print	1¼ yards	1⅞ yards	2⅛ yards
Light tan print	¾ yard	1⅛ yards	1¼ yards
Pink print #1	¾ yard	1⅝ yards	1¾ yards
Pink print #2	⅜ yard	½ yard	⅝ yard
Pink print #3	1 fat eighth	1 fat quarter★	1 fat quarter★
Brown dot	⅜ yard	⅝ yard	¾ yard
Brown print #1	1 fat eighth	1 fat quarter★	1 fat quarter★
Brown print #2	⅜ yard	½ yard	⅝ yard
Blue dot	⅞ yard	1 yard	1⅛ yards
Blue print	1 fat eighth	1 fat quarter★	1 fat quarter★
2 light green prints	⅜ yard each	⅜ yard each	½ yard each
Orange print #1	¼ yard	⅜ yard	½ yard
Orange print #2	⅜ yard	½ yard	⅝ yard
Orange stripe	¼ yard	⅜ yard	½ yard
Blue stripe	¼ yard	⅜ yard	½ yard
Backing fabric	3¾ yards	5½ yards	5½ yards
Batting	Twin-size	Full-size	Full-size

★fat quarter = 18" × 20"

Throw Size

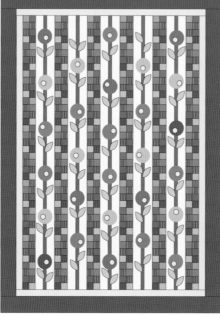

Twin Size

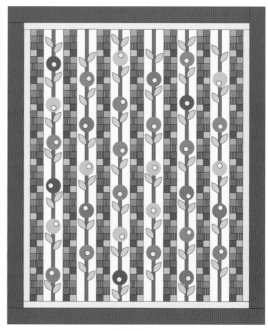

Full Size

DESIGNER

Cyndi Walker is a quilt designer and teacher living in Auburn, Washington. Her pattern company, Stitch Studios, features designs for scrap quilts using fresh colors and ideas for appliqué.

Contact her at: Stitch Studios 253-261-5942 ❋

Posy Patch
TABLE RUNNER

Size: 14" × 40"

MATERIALS

8 fat eighths★ assorted blue and
brown prints for strip sets

¼ yard light blue print for appliqué
strip

⅛ yard dark brown print for stem

2 (9") squares assorted brown prints
for leaves

3 (6") squares assorted blue prints
for flowers

1 fat eighth★ tan print for yo-yos

¼ yard blue print for binding

Paper-backed fusible web

3 (⅝"-diameter) buttons

½ yard backing fabric

18" × 44" piece of quilt batting

★fat eighth = 9" × 20"

Cutting

Measurements include ¼ " seam
allowances. Patterns for appliqué shapes
and yo-yo circles are on pages 137 and
141. Follow manufacturer's instructions
for using fusible web.

From each assorted fat eighth, cut:
• 2 (2½"-wide) strips for strip sets.

From light blue print, cut:
• 2 (3" × 32½") background strips.

From dark brown print, cut:
• 1 (1½" × 32½") stem strip.

From blue print, cut:
• 3 (2¼"-wide) strips for binding.

Quilt Assembly

NOTE: Diagrams for table runner
assembly are on page 136.

1. From assorted blue and brown print
   strips, make 2 Strip Set A and 2 Strip
   Set B. From strip sets, cut 12 (2½"-wide)
   A segments and 12 (2½"-wide) B
   segments.

2. Join 1 A segment and 1 B segment
   to make 1 strippy section. Make 12
   strippy sections.

3. Join 5 strippy sections to make 1
   strippy row. Make 2 strippy rows.

4. Add 1 (3" × 32½") light blue print
   strip to each side of 1 (1½" × 32½")
   dark brown print stem strip to make
   stem section.

5. Referring to photo, appliqué flowers
   and leaves to stem section.

6. Remove 2 squares from end of each
   remaining strippy section. Add 1
   shortened strippy section to each end
   of stem section.

7. Join strippy rows and stem section.

8. Layer backing, batting, and quilt top;
   baste. Quilt as desired.

9. Place yo-yos atop flowers as shown
   in photo. Sew a button on each yo-
   yo, stitching in place through quilt
   top and batting only.

10. Join 2¼"-wide blue print strips into
    1 continuous piece for straight-grain
    French-fold binding. Add binding to
    quilt.

Making Yo-Yos

Follow these simple steps to make yo-yos for *Autumn Posy Patch* on page 134.

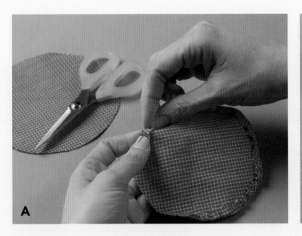

A

B

1. Cut circle using Yo-Yo Circle pattern.
2. Turn under raw edge of circle ¼" to wrong side and take small running stitches around edge through both layers *(Photo A)*. Use quilting thread or other strong thread that will not break when gathering.
3. Pull thread to gather circle with right side of fabric facing out. Make a knot to hold circle closed. Gathered side is front of yo-yo *(Photo B)*.

Sew **Smart**™
Do not make running stitches too small. Longer stitches make the circle easier to gather, and the "hole" smaller. —Marianne

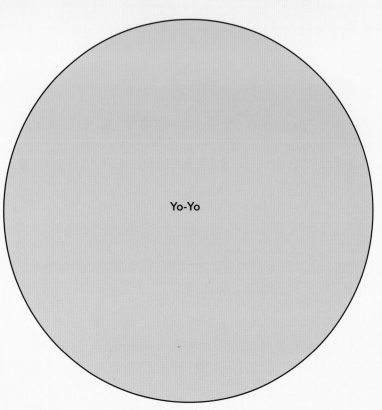

Yo-Yo

Sassy Blooms

Enjoy pretty flowers on your table any time of year with this patchwork and appliqué table runner.

Size: 14⅛" × 42½"

MATERIALS

1 fat eighth★ beige print
⅝ yard brown print
1 fat quarter★★ gold print
6 fat quarters★★ assorted purple, green, and red prints for strip sets
Paper-backed fusible web
1 yard backing fabric
18" × 46" piece of quilt batting
★fat eighth = 9" × 20"
★★fat quarter = 18" × 20"

NOTE: Fabrics in the quilt shown are from the Mementos collection by Gudrun Erla for Red Rooster Fabrics.

Cutting

Measurements include ¼" seam allowances. Patterns for appliqué pieces are on page 145. Follow manufacturer's instructions for using fusible web.

From beige print, cut:

- 1 (6½"-wide) strip. From strip, cut 3 (6½") A squares.

From brown print, cut:

- 1 (5½"-wide) strip. From strip, cut 2 (5½") squares, 2 (5⅛") squares, and 4 (4⅛") squares. Cut 5½" squares in half diagonally in both directions to make 8 quarter-square D triangles. Cut 5⅛" squares in half diagonally to make 4 half-square E triangles. Cut 4⅛" squares in half diagonally in both directions to make 16 quarter-square F triangles.
- 1 (2½"-wide) strip. From strip, cut 4 (2½") C squares.
- 4 (2¼"-wide) strips for binding.

From gold print, cut:

- 1 (3½"-wide) strip. From strip, cut 4 (3½") B squares.
- 2 (2½"-wide) strips. From strips, cut 12 (2½") C squares.

From each assorted fat quarter, cut:

- 3 (1½"-wide) strips for strip sets.

From remainder of 1 red fat quarter, cut:

- 3 Flowers.

From remainder of 1 purple fat quarter, cut:

- 3 Flower Centers.

Table Runner Assembly

1. Join 6 (1½"-wide) assorted print strips as shown in *Strip Set Diagram*. Make 3 strip sets. From strip sets, cut 12 (4½"-wide) segments.

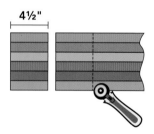

Strip Set Diagram

2. Arrange 1 Flower and 1 Flower Center on 1 beige print A square. Fuse pieces in place; machine blanket stitch using black thread. Make 3 Flower Units *(Flower Unit Diagram)*.

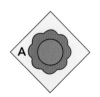

Flower Unit Diagram

3. Join 1 gold print B square and 2 brown print D triangles as shown in *Large Setting Unit Diagrams* on page 144. Make 4 Large Setting Units.

Large Setting Unit Diagrams

4. In the same manner, make 8 Small Setting Units using gold print C squares and brown print F triangles *(Small Setting Unit Diagrams)*.

Small Setting Unit Diagrams

5. Join 2 brown print C squares and 2 gold print C squares as shown in *Four-Patch Unit Diagrams*. Make 2 Four-Patch Units.

Four-Patch Unit Diagrams

6. Lay out Flower Units, strip set segments, Large and Small Setting Units, Four-Patch Units, and brown print half-square E triangles as shown in *Table Runner Assembly Diagram*.

7. Join into diagonal rows; join rows to complete table runner.

Finishing

1. Divide backing into 2 (½-yard) lengths. Join panels along short edges.

2. Layer backing, batting, and quilt top; baste. Quilt as desired. Table runner shown was quilted in the ditch, outline quilted around appliqué, and has a free-hand flower design in the strip set segments *(Quilting Diagram)*.

3. Join 2¼"-wide brown print strips into 1 continuous piece for straight-grain French-fold binding. Add binding to quilt.

Table Runner Assembly Diagram

Quilting Diagram

TRIED & TRUE

Make a dramatic statement with black-and-white and bright prints such as these from the Modern Grace collection by Windham Fabrics.

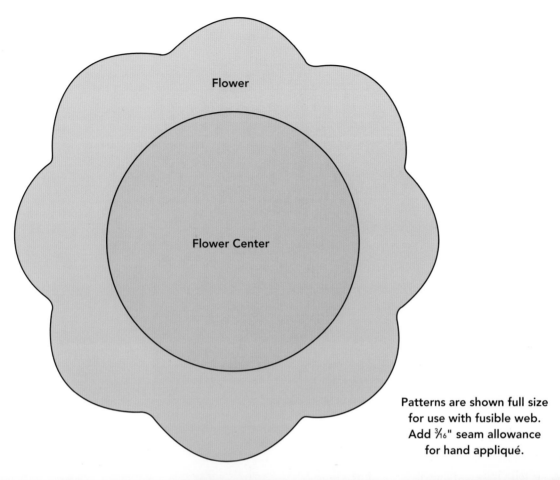

Flower

Flower Center

Patterns are shown full size
for use with fusible web.
Add ³⁄₁₆" seam allowance
for hand appliqué.

DESIGNER

Gudrun Erla was born and raised in Iceland. She moved to Minnesota in 2003, and has been designing under her design company name GE Designs—Iceland. She has published over 45 patterns and 6 books since in Minnesota and has designed several fabric collections.

Contact her at: www.gequiltdesigns.com ✳

QUILT DESIGNED AND QUILTED BY **Patti Carey**.

MADE BY **Susanne Ebsworthy**.

Gentle Spring

Wrap yourself in a cozy quilt made from flannels in the gentle colors of spring.
The baskets are pieced with mix-and-match florals, and the handle is easy appliqué.
See our *Sew Easy: Appliqué Bias Strips* on page 151.

Size: 60¾" × 75"
Blocks: 12 (10") Basket blocks

MATERIALS

3½ yards yellow floral print for
  setting squares and outer borders
½ yard green print for middle
  border
⅜ yard pink print for inner border
¾ yard pink stripe for binding
½ yard each of 6 assorted prints in
  pink, green, and cream for blocks
4½ yards backing fabric
Twin-size quilt batting

NOTE: Fabrics in the quilt shown are
from the Chapel Hill Flannel collection by
Ro Gregg for Northcott.

Cutting

Measurements include ¼" seam
allowances. Border strips are exact length
needed. You may want to make them
longer to allow for piecing variations.
Handle Placement template is on
page 149.

From yellow floral print, cut:

• 2 (15½"-wide) strips. From strips, cut
  3 (15½") squares. Cut squares in half
  diagonally in both directions to make
  12 side setting triangles (2 are extra).

• 2 (10½"-wide) strips. From strips, cut
  6 (10½") setting squares.

• 1 (8"-wide) strip. From strip, cut
  2 (8") squares. Cut squares in half
  diagonally to make 4 corner setting
  triangles.

• 8 (7½"-wide) strips. Piece strips to
  make 2 (7½" × 61½") side outer
  borders and 2 (7½" × 61¼") top and
  bottom outer borders.

From green print, cut:

• 7 (1¾"-wide) strips. Piece strips to
  make 2 (1¾" × 59") side middle
  borders and 2 (1¾" × 47¼") top and
  bottom middle borders.

From pink print, cut:

• 6 (1¼"-wide) strips. Piece strips to
  make 2 (1¼" × 57½") side inner
  borders and 2 (1¼" × 44¾") top and
  bottom inner borders.

From pink stripe, cut:

• 8 (2½"-wide) strips for binding.

From each assorted print, cut:

• 2 (8⅜") squares. Cut squares in half
  diagonally to make 4 half-square A
  triangles.

• 1 (5⅞") square. Cut square in half
  diagonally to make 2 half-square B
  triangles.

• 4 (3" × 5½") D rectangles.

• 2 (3⅜") squares. Cut squares in half
  diagonally to make 4 half-square C
  triangles.

• 2 (1½" × 11½") bias strips for basket
  handles. Refer to *Sew Easy: Appliqué
  Bias Strips* on page 151 to prepare
  strips for appliqué.

Block Assembly

1. Referring to *Handle Placement
Diagrams*, trace around Handle
Placement Template on 1 A triangle
as shown. Position 1 prepared handle
strip atop triangle as shown. Machine
appliqué using matching thread.

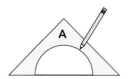 

Handle Placement Diagrams

2. Lay out handle unit and matching A triangle for basket, 1 B triangle, 2 C triangles, and 2 D rectangles as shown in *Block Assembly Diagram*. Join to complete 1 Basket block *(Block Diagram)*. Make 12 blocks.

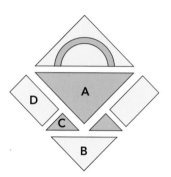

Block Assembly Diagram

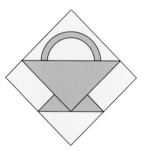

Block Diagram

Quilt Assembly

1. Lay out blocks and setting squares and triangles as shown in *Quilt Top Assembly Diagram*. Join into diagonal rows; join rows to complete quilt center.

2. Add pink print side inner borders to quilt center. Add pink print top and bottom inner borders to quilt.

3. Repeat for green print middle borders and yellow floral outer borders.

Finishing

1. Divide backing into 2 (2¼-yard) lengths. Cut 1 piece in half lengthwise to make 2 narrow panels. Join 1 narrow panel to each side of wider panel; press seam allowances toward narrow panels.

Quilt Top Assembly Diagram

2. Layer backing, batting, and quilt top; baste. Quilt as desired. Quilt shown was quilted with a rose design in the outer border and setting pieces, and with a leaf design in the middle border. The blocks are quilted in the ditch around baskets and with background stippling *(Quilting Diagram)*.

3. Join 2½"-wide pink stripe strips into 1 continuous piece for straight-grain French-fold binding. Add binding to quilt.

Quilting Diagram

SIZE OPTIONS

	Twin (75" × 89¼")	Queen (89¼" × 103½")
Blocks	20	30
MATERIALS		
Yellow Floral Print	4¼ yards	5¾ yards
Green Print	½ yard	⅝ yard
Pink Print	⅜ yard	½ yard
Pink Stripe	¾ yard	1 yard
10 Assorted Prints	½ yard each	
15 Assorted Prints		½ yard each
Backing Fabric	5½ yards	8 yards
Batting	Full-size	King-size

Twin Size

Queen Size

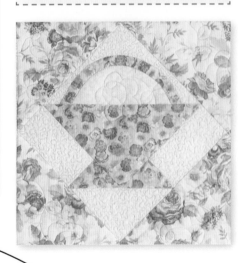

Handle Placement Template

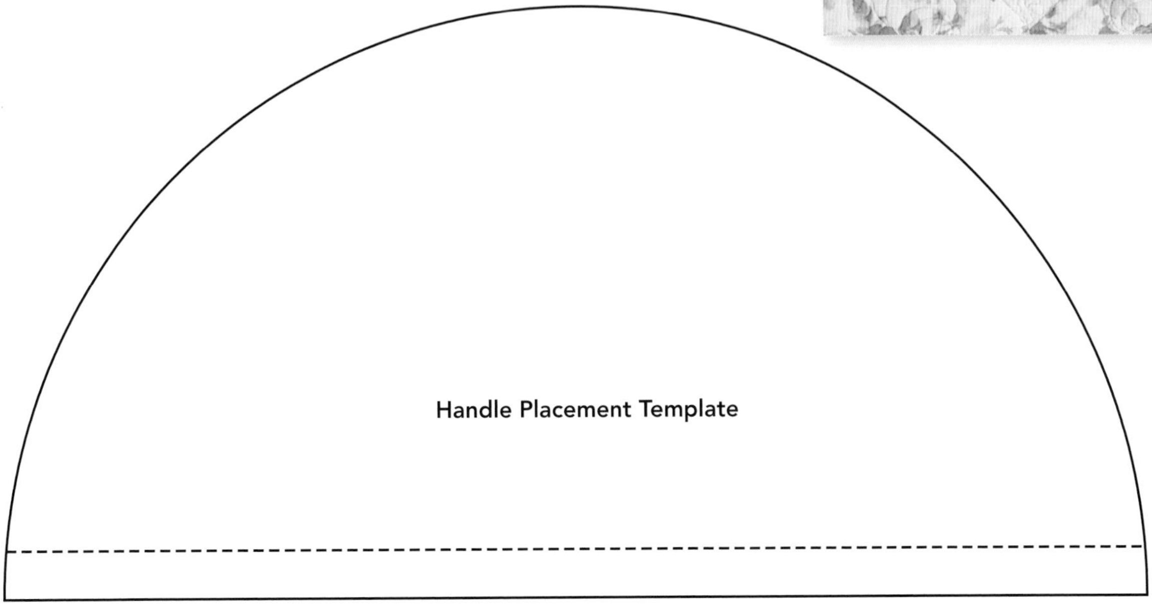

DESIGNER

Patti Carey enjoys playing with new fabrics. She loves to design quilts, and hopes to inspire other quilters with her creations.

Contact her at: patti.carey@northcott.net ☀

Appliqué Bias Strips

Use this method to prepare bias strips for basket handles.

1. Cut bias strips 3 times desired final width. For *Gentle Spring* basket handles, cut 1½" × 11½" bias strips.
2. With wrong sides together, press the strip in thirds *(Photo A)*.

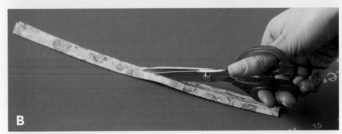

3. Trim edges of strip ³⁄₁₆" beyond pressed edges to reduce bulk *(Photo B)*.

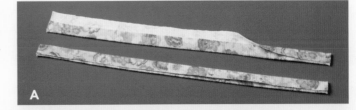

4. Mark the handle position on background piece *(Photo C)*.

5. Pin or baste handle in place over drawn line *(Photo D)*.
6. Stitch handle to background using matching thread.

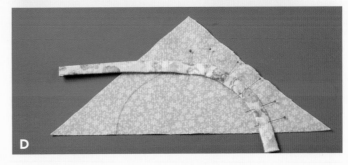

QUILT BY **Jody Houghton**.
MACHINE QUILTED BY **Linda Perry**.

Divine Vines

Leaves and vines are stitched on an easily-pieced background.
See *Sew Easy: Windowing Fusible Appliqué* on page 157 for
instructions to keep fusible appliqué soft and flexible.

Size: 46" × 58"

Blocks: 12 (12") blocks

MATERIALS

1⅜ yards blue dot for blocks and
  border

⅝ yard green check for blocks and
  binding

¾ yard green dot for blocks

¼ yard green print for blocks

1 fat quarter★ each blue check; tan
  dot; and white, purple, and yellow
  prints for blocks

Paper-backed fusible web

3 yards backing fabric

Twin-size quilt batting

★ fat quarter = 18" × 20"

NOTE: Fabrics in the quilt shown are
from the Sisterhood of Quilters collection
by Jody Houghton for Lyndhurst Studio.

Cutting

Measurements include ¼" seam
allowances. Border strips are exact
length needed. You may want to make
them longer to allow for piecing
variations. Pattern for Leaf is on page
155. Follow manufacturer's instructions
for using fusible web.

From blue dot, cut:

• 5 (5½"-wide) strips. Piece strips to
  make 2 (5½" × 48½") side borders
  and 2 (5½" × 46½") top and bottom
  borders.

• 6 (2½"-wide) strips. From strips, cut
  12 (2½" × 12½") A rectangles and
  6 (2½" × 8½") E rectangles.

From green check, cut:

• 2 (2½"-wide) strips. From strips, cut
  6 (2½" × 8½") E rectangles.

• 6 (2¼"-wide) strips for binding.

From green dot, cut:

• 6 (2½"-wide) strips. From strips, cut
  12 (2½" × 12½") A rectangles and
  6 (2½" × 10½") D rectangles.

• 12 Leaves.

• 2 Leaves reversed.

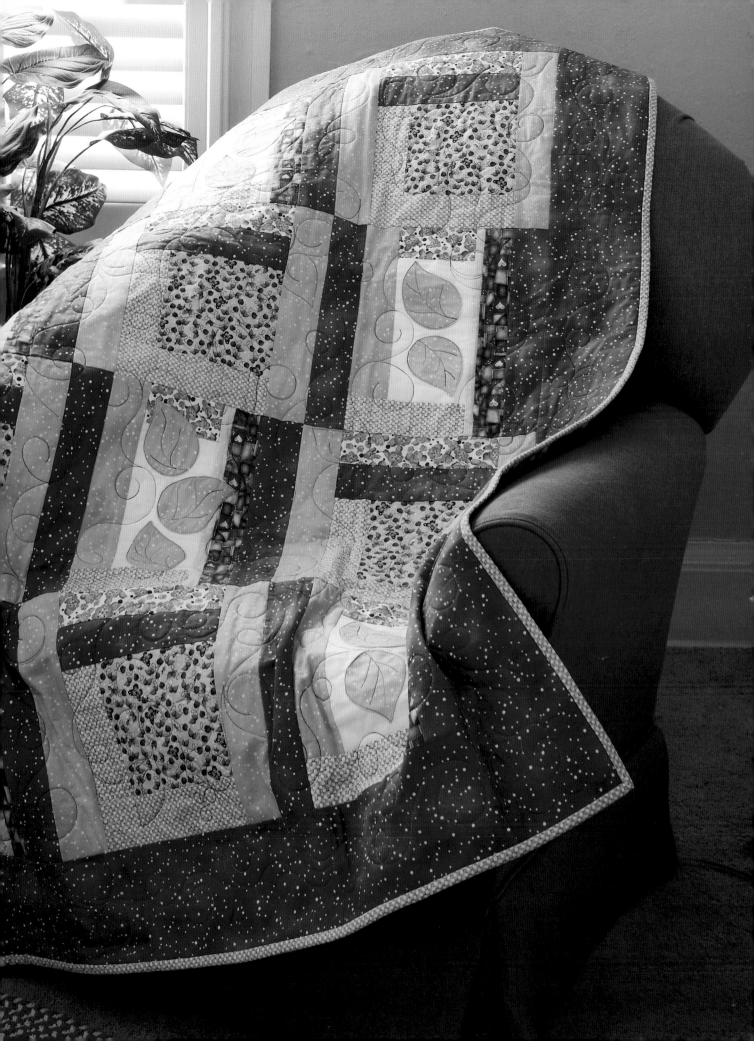

From green print, cut:

- 1 (6½"-wide) strip. From strip, cut 6 (6½") I squares.

From blue check fat quarter, cut:

- 6 (2½"-wide) strips. From strips, cut 12 (2½" × 6½") F rectangles.

From tan dot fat quarter, cut:

- 6 (1"-wide) strips. From strips, cut 6 (1" × 12½") C rectangles.

From white print fat quarter, cut:

- 3 (4½"-wide) strips. From strips, cut 6 (4½" × 8½") H rectangles.

From purple print fat quarter, cut:

- 1 (12½"-wide) strip. From strip, cut 6 (12½" × 2") B rectangles.

From yellow print, cut:

- 5 (2½"-wide) strips. From strips, cut 6 (2½" × 8½") E rectangles and 6 (2½" × 4½") G rectangles.

Block Assembly

1. Lay out 1 white print H rectangle, 1 yellow print G rectangle, 1 green dot D rectangle, 1 blue check F rectangle, 1 tan dot C rectangle, 1 purple print B rectangle, and 2 blue dot A rectangles as shown in *Block 1 Assembly Diagram*. Join rectangles to make 1 Block 1 background (*Block 1 Diagram*).

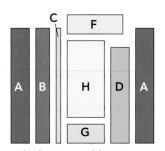

Block 1 Assembly Diagram

Block 1 Diagram

2. Referring to photo on page 156, position 2 leaves atop block background. Fuse and machine appliqué leaves in place.

3. Machine stitch veins on leaves using green thread as shown in Leaf pattern on page 155. Make 6 Block 1. **NOTE:** 2 blocks have 3 leaves.

4. Lay out 1 green print I square, 1 blue check F rectangle, 1 green check E rectangle, 1 blue dot E rectangle, 1 yellow print E rectangle, and 2 green dot A rectangles as shown in *Block 2 Assembly Diagram*. Join to complete 1 Block 2 (*Block 2 Diagram*). Make 6 Block 2.

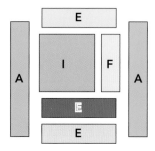

Block 2 Assembly Diagram

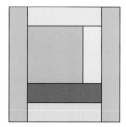

Block 2 Diagram

Quilt Assembly

1. Lay out blocks as shown in *Quilt Top Assembly Diagram*. Join blocks into rows; join rows to complete quilt center.

2. Add blue dot side borders to quilt center. Add blue dot top and bottom borders to quilt.

Finishing

1. Divide backing into 2 (1½-yard) lengths. Join panels lengthwise. Seam will run horizontally.

2. Layer backing, batting, and quilt top; baste. Quilt as desired. Quilt shown was quilted with an overall design of vines and leaves (*Quilting Diagram*).

3. Join 2¼"-wide green check strips into 1 continuous piece for straight-grain French-fold binding. Add binding to quilt.

Quilting Diagram

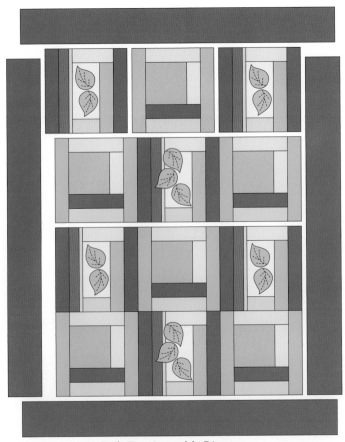

Quilt Top Assembly Diagram

Pattern is shown full
size and is reversed for use
with fusible web. Add $^3/_{16}$" seam
allowance for hand appliqué.

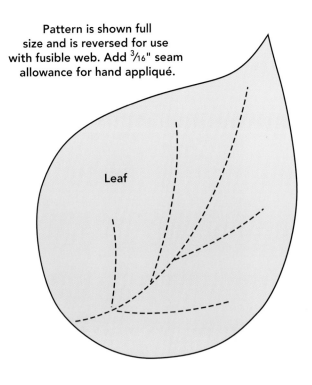

Leaf

SIZE OPTIONS

	Crib (34" × 46")	Twin (70" × 94")	Full (82" × 106")
Block 1	3	18	24
Block 2	3	17	24
Setting	2 × 3	5 × 7	6 × 8

MATERIALS

	Crib (34" × 46")	Twin (70" × 94")	Full (82" × 106")
Blue Dot	1 yard	2⅝ yards	3¼ yards
Green Check	½ yard	1 yard	1½ yards
Green Dot	½ yard	2 yards	2½ yards
Green Print	¼ yard	¾ yard	1 yard
Blue Check	1 fat quarter	½ yard	¾ yard
Tan Dot	1 fat quarter	¼ yard	⅜ yard
White Print	1 fat quarter	¾ yard	1 yard
Purple Print	1 fat quarter	½ yard	½ yard
Yellow Print	1 fat quarter	¾ yard	¾ yard
Backing Fabric	1½ yards	6 yards	7½ yards
Batting	Crib-size	Full-size	Queen-size

WEB EXTRA
Go to www.FonsandPorter.com/divinevinessizes to download *Quilt Top Assembly Diagrams* for these size options.

DESIGNER

Jody's love of sewing was established as a young girl making doll clothes and stuffed animals from scraps of fabric that her mom had from making clothes for Jody and her two sisters. Childhood play became a profession in 1982, when she established Jody Houghton Designs, Inc., creating gift products from her artwork. Her business motto is "Creating a Life, while Creating a Living."

Contact her at: 5434 River Rd N #135, Keizer, OR 97303 • (503) 656-7748

Jody@jodyhoughton.com • www.sisterhoodofquilters.com ❋

Windowing Fusible Appliqué

Choose a lightweight "sewable" fusible product. The staff at your favorite quilt shop can recommend brands. Always read and follow manufacturer's instructions for proper fusing time and iron temperature.

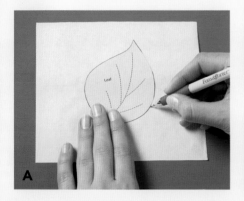

A

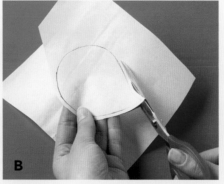

B

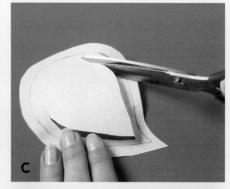

C

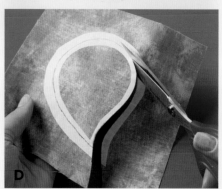

D

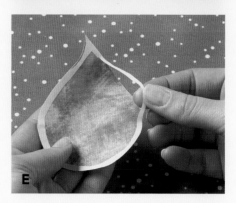

E

> ## Sew Smart™
> Fused shapes will be the reverse of the pattern you trace. If it's important for an object to face a certain direction, make a reverse pattern to trace. We do this quickly by tracing the design on tracing paper, then turning the paper over and tracing the design through onto the other side of the paper.
> —Liz

1. Use a pencil to trace appliqué motifs onto paper side of fusible web, making a separate tracing for each appliqué needed (Photo A).

2. Roughly cut out drawn appliqué shapes, cutting about ¼" outside drawn lines (Photo B).

3. "Window" fusible by trimming out the interior of the shape, leaving a scant ¼" inside drawn line (Photo C). Follow manufacturer's instructions to fuse web side of each shape to wrong side of appliqué fabric.

4. Cut out appliqués, cutting carefully on drawn outline (Photo D). Only a thin band of fusible web frames the shape.

5. Peel off paper backing (Photo E). Position appliqué in place on background fabric, and follow manufacturer's instructions to fuse shapes in place.

> ## Sew Smart™
> If you have trouble peeling the paper backing, try scoring paper with a pin to give you an edge to begin with. —Marianne

QUILT BY **Lori Hein**.

MACHINE QUILTED BY **Wanda Jeffries**.

Bandana Beauty

Use a traditional bandana print in classic trefoil and paisley shapes to make this easy appliqué quilt.

Size: 56" × 72"

MATERIALS

1¼ yards red print for blocks and appliqué

1¼ yards blue print for blocks and appliqué

2½ yards cream print for background (must be at least 40½" wide)

¾ yard dark red print for blocks and appliqué

1 yard dark blue print for blocks, appliqué, and binding

Paper-backed fusible web

Dark blue perle cotton

3½ yards backing fabric

Twin-size quilt batting

NOTE: Fabrics in the quilt shown are from the Bandana Beauties (Classics) collection by Benartex, Inc.

Cutting

Measurements include ¼" seam allowances. Patterns for appliqué pieces are on pages 162–163. Follow manufacturer's instructions for using fusible web.

From red print, cut:

• 3 (8½"-wide) strips. From strips, cut 9 (8½") F squares.

• 4 A.

• 8 D.

From blue print, cut:

• 3 (8½"-wide) strips. From strips, cut 11 (8½") F squares.

• 8 B.

• 8 B reversed.

From cream print, cut:

• 1 (40½"-wide) strip. From strip, cut 1 (40½") square.

• 5 (4½"-wide) strips. From strips, cut 36 (4½") G squares.

• 9 (2½"-wide) strips. From strips, cut 144 (2½") H squares.

From dark red print, cut:

• 3 (4½"-wide) strips. From strips, cut 18 (4½") G squares.

• 8 C.

From dark blue print, cut:

• 3 (4½"-wide) strips. From strips, cut 18 (4½") G squares.

• 7 (2¼"-wide) strips for binding.

• 8 E.

Center Assembly

1. Referring to *Appliqué Placement Diagram,* lay out appliqué pieces on cream print background square. Fuse in place.

> ### Sew **Smart**™
>
> Fold and lightly press background square into quadrants and then in half diagonally. Use fold lines for accurate placement of appliqué pieces (*Appliqué Placement Diagram*).
> —Marianne

Appliqué Placement Diagram

2. Using matching thread, zigzag stitch around appliqué pieces.

3. Referring to *Quilt Top Assembly Diagram,* mark lines connecting dark blue E pieces using Marking Template on page 162. Using dark blue perle cotton, stem stitch on lines (*Stem Stitch Diagram*).

Stem Stitch Diagram

Block Assembly

1. Referring to *Diagonal Seams Diagrams,* place 1 cream print H square atop 1 dark blue print G square, right sides facing. Stitch diagonally from corner to corner as shown. Trim ¼" beyond stitching. Press open to reveal triangle. Repeat

Diagonal Seams Diagrams

for 3 remaining corners to complete 1 blue Square-in-a-Square Unit. Make 18 blue Square-in-a-Square Units.

2. In the same manner, make 18 red Square-in-a-Square Units using cream print H squares and dark red print G squares.

3. Lay out 2 cream print G squares, 1 red Square-in-a-Square Unit and 1 blue Square-in-a-Square Unit as shown in *Block Assembly Diagram.* Join to complete 1 block (*Block Diagram*). Make 18 blocks.

Quilt Top Assembly Diagram

Block Assembly
Diagram

Block Diagram

Quilt Assembly

1. Lay out center unit, F squares, and blocks as shown in *Quilt Top Assembly Diagram*.

2. Join into rows; join rows to complete quilt top.

Finishing

1. Divide backing into 2 (1¾-yard) lengths. Join panels lengthwise. Seam will run horizontally.

2. Layer backing, batting, and quilt top; baste. Quilt as desired. Quilt shown

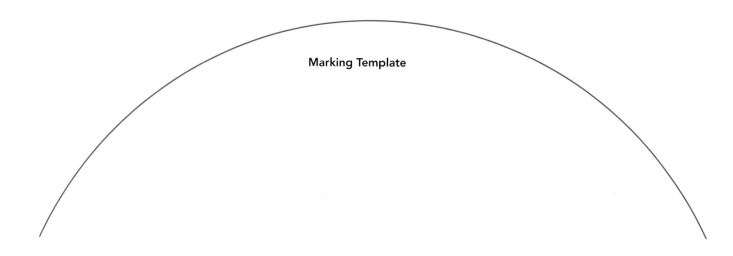

Marking Template

was outline quilted around appliqué and has an allover swirl design in the red and blue A squares and cream print background *(Quilting Diagram)*.

3. Join 2¼"-wide dark blue print strips into 1 continuous piece for straight-grain French-fold binding. Add binding to quilt.

Patterns are shown full size for use with fusible web. Add ³⁄₁₆" seam allowance for hand appliqué.

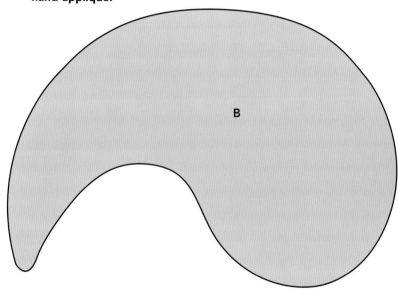

B

Quilting Diagram

DESIGNER

Lori Hein was introduced to quilting in 1983, when she was a young mother of three living on her husband's family homestead near Spokane, Washington. She immediately loved working with the fabrics and block designs. When her children were nearly raised, Lori began working at a quilt shop, teaching classes, and designing her own quilt patterns. In 2005, she launched her Web site company, Cool Water Quilts.

Contact her at: lori@coolwaterquilts.com • www.coolwaterquilts.com ✳

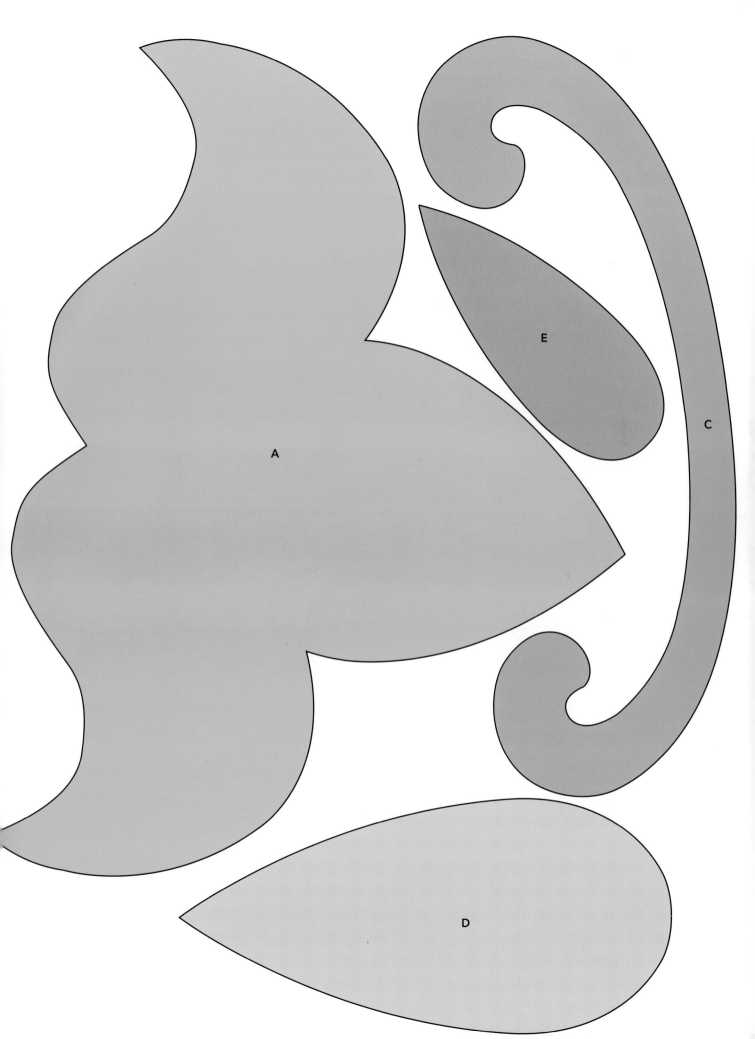

General Instructions

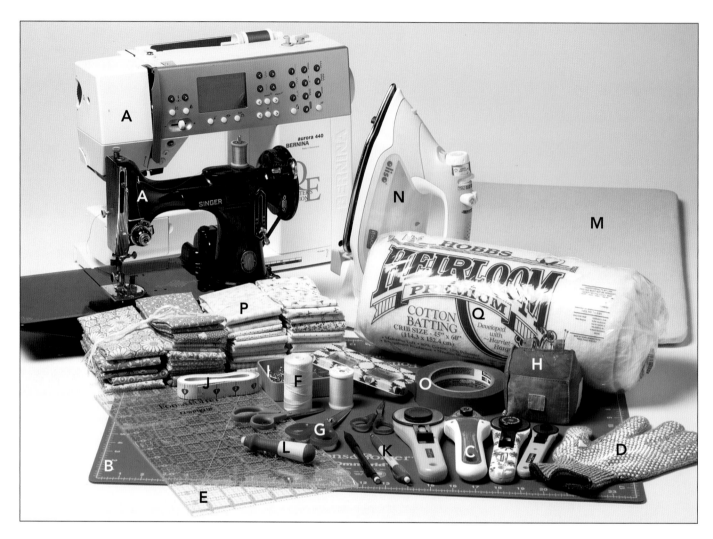

Basic Supplies

You'll need a **sewing machine (A)** in good working order to construct patchwork blocks, join blocks together, add borders, and machine quilt. We encourage you to purchase a machine from a local dealer, who can help you with service in the future, rather than from a discount store. Another option may be to borrow a machine from a friend or family member. If the machine has not been used in a while, have it serviced by a local dealer to make sure it is in good working order. If you need an extension cord, one with a surge protector is a good idea.

A **rotary cutting mat (B)** is essential for accurate and safe rotary cutting. Purchase one that is no smaller than 18" × 24".

Rotary cutting mats are made of "self-healing" material that can be used over and over.

A **rotary cutter (C)** is a cutting tool that looks like a pizza cutter, and has a very sharp blade. We recommend starting with a standard size 45mm rotary cutter. Always lock or close your cutter when it is not in use, and keep it out of the reach of children.

A **safety glove** (also known as a *Klutz Glove)* **(D)** is also recommended. Wear your safety glove on the hand that is holding the ruler in place. Because it is made of cut-resistant material, the safety glove protects your non-cutting hand from accidents that can occur if your cutting hand slips while cutting.

An acrylic **ruler (E)** is used in combination with your cutting mat and rotary cutter. We recommend the Fons & Porter

8" × 14" ruler, but a 6" × 12" ruler is another good option. You'll need a ruler with inch, quarter-inch, and eighth-inch markings that show clearly for ease of measuring. Choose a ruler with 45-degree-angle, 30-degree-angle, and 60-degree-angle lines marked on it as well.

Since you will be using 100% cotton fabric for your quilts, use **cotton or cotton-covered polyester thread (F)** for piecing and quilting. Avoid 100% polyester thread, as it tends to snarl.

Keep a pair of small **scissors (G)** near your sewing machine for cutting threads.

Thin, good quality **straight pins (H)** are preferred by quilters. The pins included with pin cushions are normally too thick to use for piecing, so discard them. Purchase a box of nickel-plated brass **safety pins** size #1 **(I)** to use for pin-basting the layers of your quilt together for machine quilting.

Invest in a 120"-long dressmaker's **measuring tape (J)**. This will come in handy when making borders for your quilt.

A 0.7–0.9mm mechanical **pencil (K)** works well for marking on your fabric.

Invest in a quality sharp **seam ripper (L)**. Every quilter gets well-acquainted with her seam ripper!

Set up an **ironing board (M)** and **iron (N)** in your sewing area. Pressing yardage before cutting, and pressing patchwork seams as you go are both essential for quality quiltmaking. Select an iron that has steam capability.

Masking **tape (O)** or painter's tape works well to mark your sewing machine so you can sew an accurate ¼" seam. You will also use tape to hold your backing fabric taut as you prepare your quilt sandwich for machine quilting.

The most exciting item that you will need for quilting is **fabric (P)**. Quilters generally prefer 100% cotton fabrics for their quilts. This fabric is woven from cotton threads, and has a lengthwise and a crosswise grain. The term "bias" is used to describe the diagonal grain of the fabric. If you make a 45-degree angle cut through a square of cotton fabric, the cut edges will be bias edges, which are quite stretchy. As you learn more quiltmaking techniques, you'll learn how bias can work to your advantage or disadvantage.

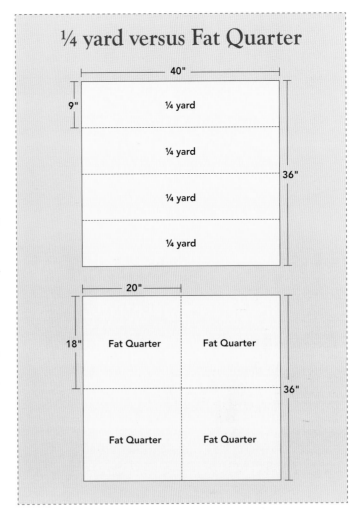

¼ yard versus Fat Quarter

Fabric is sold by the yard at quilt shops and fabric stores. Quilting fabric is generally about 40"–44" wide, so a yard is about 40" wide by 36" long. As you collect fabrics to build your own personal stash, you will buy yards, half yards (about 18" × 40"), quarter yards (about 9" × 40"), as well as other lengths.

Many quilt shops sell "fat quarters," a special cut favored by quilters. A fat quarter is created by cutting a half yard down the fold line into two 18" × 20" pieces (fat quarters) that are sold separately. Quilters like the nearly square shape of the fat quarter because it is more useful than the narrow regular quarter yard cut.

Batting (Q) is the filler between quilt top and backing that makes your quilt a quilt. It can be cotton, polyester, cotton-polyester blend, wool, silk, or other natural materials, such as bamboo or corn. Make sure the batting you buy is at least six inches wider and six inches longer than your quilt top.

Accurate Cutting

Measuring and cutting accuracy are important for successful quilting. Measure at least twice, and cut once!

Cut strips across the fabric width unless directed otherwise.

Cutting for patchwork usually begins with cutting strips, which are then cut into smaller pieces. First, cut straight strips from a fat quarter:

1. Fold fat quarter in half with selvage edge at the top (*Photo A*).

2. Straighten edge of fabric by placing ruler atop fabric, aligning one of the lines on ruler with selvage edge of fabric (*Photo B*). Cut along right edge of ruler.

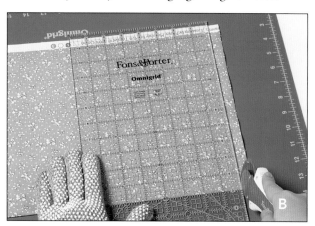

3. Rotate fabric, and use ruler to measure from cut edge to desired strip width (*Photo C*). Measurements in instructions include ¼" seam allowances.

4. After cutting the required number of strips, cut strips into squares and label them.

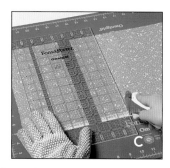

Setting up Your Sewing Machine

Sew Accurate ¼" Seams

Standard seam width for patchwork and quiltmaking is ¼". Some machines come with a patchwork presser foot, also known as a quarter-inch foot. If your machine doesn't have a quarter-inch foot, you may be able to purchase one from a dealer. Or, you can create a quarter-inch seam guide on your machine using masking tape or painter's tape.

Place an acrylic ruler on your sewing machine bed under the presser foot. Slowly turn handwheel until the tip of the needle barely rests atop the ruler's quarter-inch mark (*Photo A*). Make sure the lines on the ruler are parallel to the lines on the machine throat plate. Place tape on the machine bed along edge of ruler (*Photo B*).

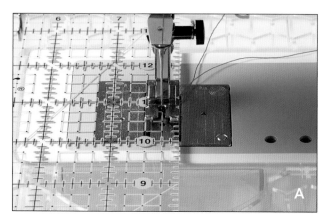

Take a Simple Seam Test

Seam accuracy is critical to machine piecing, so take this simple test once you have your quarter-inch presser foot on your machine or have created a tape guide.

Place 2 (2½") squares right sides together, and sew with a scant ¼" seam. Open squares and finger press seam. To finger press, with right sides facing you, press the seam to one side with your fingernail. Measure across pieces, raw edge to raw edge (*Photo C*). If they measure 4½", you have passed the test! Repeat the test as needed to make sure you can confidently sew a perfect ¼" seam.

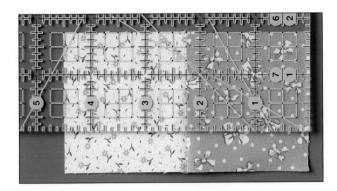

Sewing Comfortably

Other elements that promote pleasant sewing are good lighting, a comfortable chair, background music—and chocolate! Good lighting promotes accurate sewing. The better you can see what you are working on, the better your results. A comfortable chair enables you to sew for longer periods of time. An office chair with a good back rest and adjustable height works well. Music helps keep you relaxed. Chocolate is, for many quilters, simply a necessity.

Tips for Patchwork and Pressing

As you sew more patchwork, you'll develop your own shortcuts and favorite methods. Here are a few favored by many quilters:

- As you join patchwork units to form rows, and join rows to form blocks, press seams in opposite directions from row to row whenever possible (*Photo A*). By pressing seams one direction in the first row and the opposite direction in the next row, you will often create seam allowances that abut when rows are joined (*Photo B*). Abutting or nesting seams are ideal for forming perfectly matched corners on the right side of your quilt blocks and quilt top. Such pressing is not always possible, so don't worry if you end up with seam allowances facing the same direction as you join units.

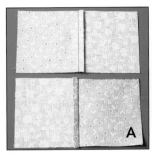 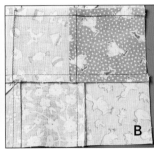

- Sew on and off a small, folded fabric square to prevent bobbin thread from bunching at throat plate (*Photo C*). You'll also save thread, which means fewer stops to wind bobbins, and fewer hanging threads to be snipped. Repeated use of the small piece of fabric gives it lots of thread "legs," so some quilters call it a spider.

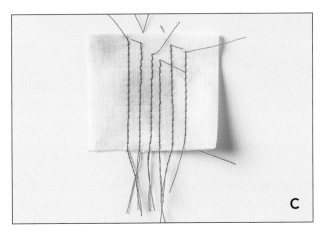

● Chain piece patchwork to reduce the amount of thread you use, and minimize the number and length of threads you need to trim from patchwork. Without cutting threads at the end of a seam, take 3–4 stitches without any fabric under the needle, creating a short thread chain approximately ⅛" long (*Photo D*). Repeat until you have a long line of pieces. Remove chain from machine, clip threads between units, and press seams.

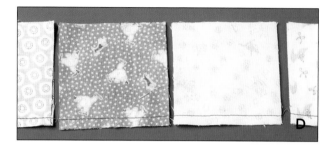

● Trim off tiny triangle tips (sometimes called dog ears) created when making triangle-square units (*Photo E*). Trimming triangles reduces bulk and makes patchwork units and blocks lie flatter. Though no one will see the back of your quilt top once it's quilted, a neat back free of dangling threads and patchwork points is the mark of a good quilter. Also, a smooth, flat quilt top is easier to quilt, whether by hand or machine.

● Careful pressing will make your patchwork neat and crisp, and will help make your finished quilt top lie flat. Ironing and pressing are two different skills. Iron fabric to remove wrinkles using a back and forth, smoothing motion. Press patchwork and quilt blocks by raising and gently lowering the iron atop your work. After sewing a patchwork unit, first press the seam with the unit closed, pressing to set, or embed, the stitching. Setting the seam this way will help produce straight, crisp seams. Open the unit and press on the right side with the seam toward the darkest fabric,

being careful to not form a pleat in your seam, and carefully pressing the patchwork flat.

● Many quilters use finger pressing to open and flatten seams of small units before pressing with an iron. To finger press, open patchwork unit with right side of fabric facing you. Run your fingernail firmly along seam, making sure unit is fully open with no pleat.

● Careful use of steam in your iron will make seams and blocks crisp and flat (*Photo F*). Aggressive ironing can stretch blocks out of shape, and is a common pitfall for new quilters.

Adding Borders

Follow these simple instructions to make borders that fit perfectly on your quilt.

1. Find the length of your quilt by measuring through the quilt center, not along the edges, since the edges may have stretched. Take 3 measurements and average them to determine the length to cut your side borders (*Diagram A*). Cut 2 side borders this length.

2. Fold border strips in half to find center. Pinch to create crease mark or place a pin at center. Fold quilt top in half crosswise to find center of side. Attach side borders to quilt center by pinning them at the ends and the center, and easing in any fullness. If quilt edge is a bit longer than border, pin and sew with border on top; if border is

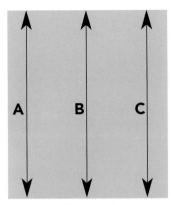

Diagram A

A _____

B _____

C _____

TOTAL _____

_____ ÷3

AVERAGE
LENGTH _____

HELPFUL TIP
Use the following decimal conversions to calculate
your quilt's measurements:

⅛" = .125	⅝" = .625
¼" = .25	¾" = .75
⅜" = .375	⅞" = .875
½" = .5	

slightly longer than quilt top, pin and sew with border on the bottom. Machine feed dogs will ease in the fullness of the longer piece. Press seams toward borders.

3. Find the width of your quilt by measuring across the quilt and side borders (*Diagram B*). Take 3 measurements and average them to determine the length to cut your top and bottom borders. Cut 2 borders this length.

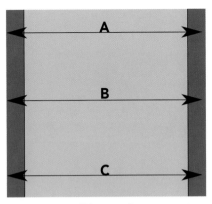

Diagram B

4. Mark centers of borders and top and bottom edges of quilt top. Attach top and bottom borders to quilt, pinnning at ends and center, and easing in any fullness (*Diagram C*). Press seams toward borders.

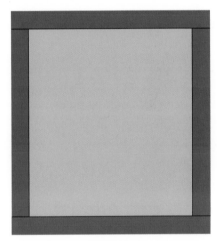

Diagram C

5. Gently steam press entire quilt top on one side and then the other. When pressing on wrong side, trim off any loose threads.

Joining Border Strips

Not all quilts have borders, but they are a nice complement to a quilt top. If your border is longer than 40", you will need to join 2 or more strips to make a border the required length. You can join border strips with either a straight seam parallel to the ends of the strips (*Photo A*), or with a diagonal seam. For the diagonal seam method, place one border strip perpendicular to another strip, rights sides facing (*Photo B*). Stitch diagonally across strips as shown. Trim seam allowance to ¼". Press seam open (*Photo C*).

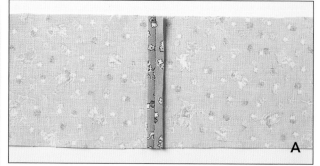

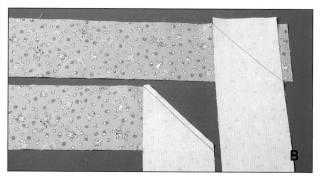

Quilting Your Quilt

Quilters today joke that there are three ways to quilt a quilt—by hand, by machine, or by check. Some enjoy making quilt tops so much, they prefer to hire a professional machine quilter to finish their work. The Split Nine Patch baby quilt shown at left has simple machine quilting that you can do yourself.

Decide what color thread will look best on your quilt top before choosing your backing fabric. A thread color that will blend in with the quilt top is a good choice for beginners. Choose backing fabric that will blend with your thread as well. A print fabric is a good choice for hiding less-than-perfect machine quilting. The backing fabric must be at least 3"–4" larger than your quilt top on all 4 sides. For example: if your quilt top measures 44" × 44", your backing needs to be at least 50" × 50". If your quilt top is 80" × 96", then your backing fabric needs to be at least 86" × 102".

For quilt tops 36" wide or less, use a single width of fabric for the backing. Buy enough length to allow adequate margin at quilt edges, as noted above. When your quilt is wider than 36", one option is to use 60"-, 90"-, or 108"-wide fabric for the quilt backing. Because fabric selection is limited for wide fabrics, quilters generally piece the quilt backing from 44/45"-wide fabric. Plan on 40"–42" of usable fabric width when estimating how much fabric to purchase. Plan your piecing strategy to avoid having a seam along the vertical or horizontal center of the quilt.

For a quilt 37"–60" wide, a backing with horizontal seams is usually the most economical use of fabric. For example, for a quilt 50" × 70", vertical seams would require 152", or 4¼ yards, of 44/45"-wide fabric (76" + 76" = 152"). Horizontal seams would require 112", or 3¼ yards (56" + 56" = 112").

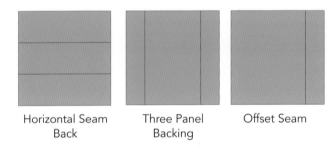

Horizontal Seam Back   Three Panel Backing   Offset Seam

For a quilt 61"–80" wide, most quilters piece a three-panel backing, with vertical seams, from two lengths of fabric. Cut one of the pieces in half lengthwise, and sew the halves to opposite sides of the wider panel. Press the seams away from the center panel.

For a quilt 81"–120" wide, you will need three lengths of fabric, plus extra margin. For example, for a quilt 108" × 108", purchase at least 342", or 9½ yards, of 44/45"-wide fabric (114" + 114" + 114" = 342").

For a three-panel backing, pin the selvage edge of the enter panel to the selvage edge of the side panel, with edges aligned and right sides facing. Machine stitch with a ½" seam. Trim seam allowances to ¼", trimming off the selvages from both panels at once. Press the seam away from the center of the quilt. Repeat on other side of center panel.

For a two-panel backing, join panels in the same manner as above, and press the seam to one side.

Create a "quilt sandwich" by layering your backing, batting, and quilt top. Find the crosswise center of the backing fabric by folding it in half. Mark with a pin on each side. Lay backing down on a table or floor, wrong side up. Tape corners and edges of backing to the surface with masking or painter's tape so that backing is taut (*Photo A*).

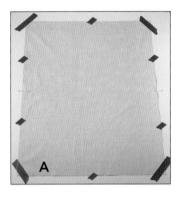

Fold batting in half crosswise and position it atop backing fabric, centering folded edge at center of backing (*Photo B*). Unfold batting and smooth it out atop backing (*Photo C*).

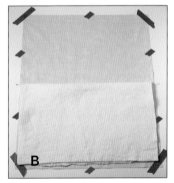
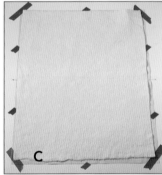

In the same manner, fold the quilt top in half crosswise and center it atop backing and batting (*Photo D*). Unfold top and smooth it out atop batting (*Photo E*).

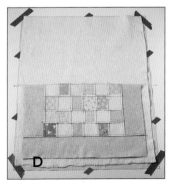

Use safety pins to pin baste the layers (*Photo F*). Pins should be about a fist width apart. A special tool, called a Kwik Klip, or a grapefruit spoon makes closing the pins easier. As you slide a pin through all three layers, slide the point of the pin into one of the tool's grooves. Push on the tool to help close the pin.

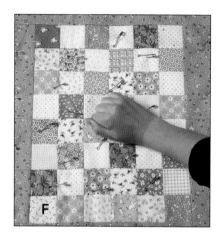

For straight line quilting, install an even feed or walking foot on your machine. This presser foot helps all three layers of your quilt move through the machine evenly without bunching.

Walking Foot

Stitching "in the ditch"

An easy way to quilt your first quilt is to stitch "in the ditch" along seam lines. No marking is needed for this type of quilting.

Binding Your Quilt

Preparing Binding

Strips for quilt binding may be cut either on the straight of grain or on the bias. For the quilts in this booklet, cut strips on the straight of grain.

1. Measure the perimeter of your quilt and add approximately 24" to allow for mitered corners and finished ends.

2. Cut the number of strips necessary to achieve desired length. We like to cut binding strips 2¼" wide.

3. Join your strips with diagonal seams into 1 continuous piece (*Photo A*). Press the seams open. (See page 169 for instructions for the diagonal seams method of joining strips.)

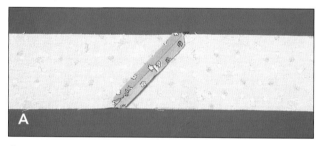

4. Press your binding in half lengthwise, with wrong sides facing, to make French-fold binding (*Photo B*).

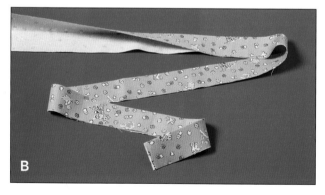

Attaching Binding

Attach the binding to your quilt using an even-feed or walking foot. This prevents puckering when sewing through the three layers.

1. Choose beginning point along one side of quilt. Do not start at a corner. Match the two raw edges of the binding strip to the raw edge of the quilt top. The folded edge

will be free and to left of seam line (*Photo C*). Leave 12" or longer tail of binding strip dangling free from beginning point. Stitch, using ¼" seam, through all layers.

2. For mitered corners, stop stitching ¼" from corner; backstitch, and remove quilt from sewing machine (*Photo D*). Place a pin ¼" from corner to mark where you will stop stitching.

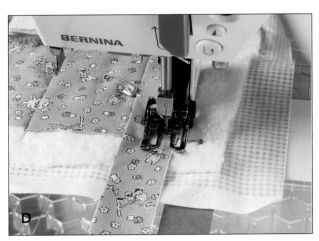

Rotate quilt quarter turn and fold binding straight up, away from corner, forming 45-degree-angle fold (*Photo E*).

Bring binding straight down in line with next edge to be sewn, leaving top fold even with raw edge of previously sewn side (*Photo F*). Begin stitching at top edge, sewing through all layers (*Photo G*).

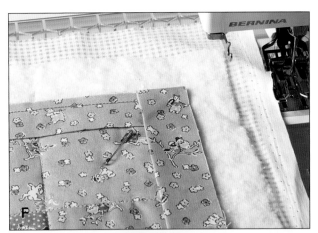

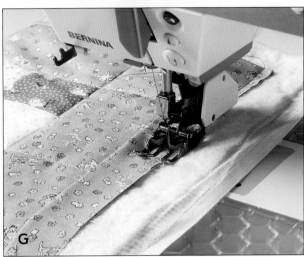

3. To finish binding, stop stitching about 8" away from starting point, leaving about a 12" tail at end (*Photo H*). Bring beginning and end of binding to center of 8" opening and fold each back, leaving about ¼" space

between the two folds of binding (*Photo I*). (Allowing this ¼" extra space is critical, as binding tends to stretch when it is stitched to the quilt. If the folded ends meet at this point, your binding will be too long for the space after the ends are joined.) Crease folds of binding with your fingernail.

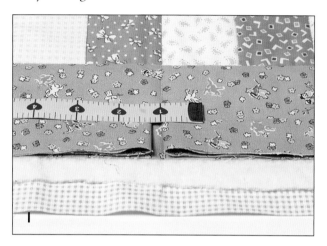

4. Open out each edge of binding and draw line across wrong side of binding on creased fold line, as shown in *Photo J*. Draw line along lengthwise fold of binding at same spot to create an X (*Photo K*).

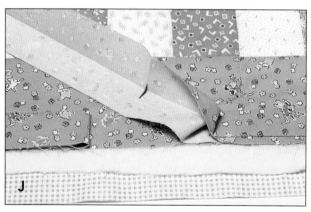

5. With edge of ruler at marked X, line up 45-degree-angle marking on ruler with one long side of binding (*Photo L*). Draw diagonal line across binding as shown in *Photo M*.

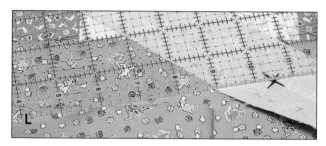

Repeat for other end of binding. Lines must angle in same direction (*Photo N*).

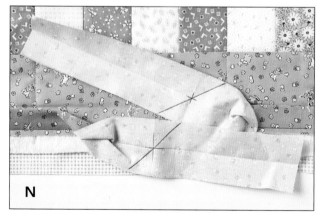

6. Pin binding ends together with right sides facing, pin-matching diagonal lines as shown in *Photo O*. Binding ends will be at right angles to each other. Machine-stitch along diagonal line, removing pins as you stitch (*Photo P*).

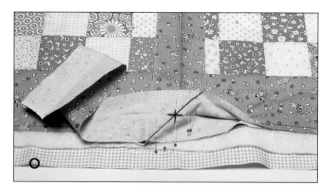

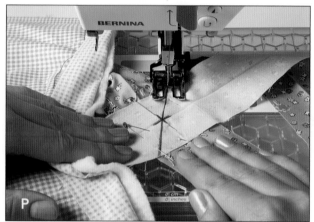

7. Lay binding against quilt to double-check that it is correct length (*Photo Q*). Trim ends of binding ¼" from diagonal seam (*Photo R*).

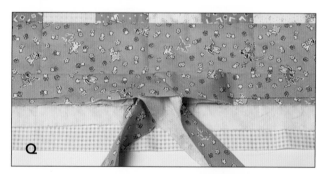

8. Finger press diagonal seam open (*Photo S*). Fold binding in half and finish stitching binding to quilt (*Photo T*).

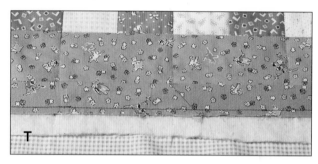

Hand Stitching Binding to Quilt Back

1. Trim any excess batting and quilt back with scissors or a rotary cutter (*Photo A*). Leave enough batting (about ⅛" beyond quilt top) to fill binding uniformly when it is turned to quilt back.

2. Bring folded edge of binding to quilt back so that it covers machine stitching. Blindstitch folded edge to quilt backing, using a few pins just ahead of stitching to hold binding in place (*Photo B*).

3. Continue stitching to corner. Fold unstitched binding from next side under, forming a 45-degree angle and a mitered corner. Stitch mitered folds on both front and back (*Photo C*).

Finishing Touches

● **Label your quilt so the recipient and future generations know who made it.** To make a label, use a fabric marking pen to write the details on a small piece of solid color fabric (*Photo A*). To make writing easier, put pieces of masking tape on the wrong side. Remove tape after writing. Use your iron to turn under ¼" on each edge, then stitch the label to the back of your quilt using a blindstitch, taking care not to sew through to quilt top.

● **Take a photo of your quilt.** Keep your photos in an album or journal along with notes, fabric swatches, and other information about the quilts.

● **If your quilt is a gift, include care instructions.** Some quilt shops carry pre-printed care labels you can sew onto the quilt (*Photo B*). Or, make a care label using the method described above.